Motorcycle Journeys Through the

Pacific Northwest

by Bruce Hansen

Whitehorse Press
Center Conway, New Hampshire

Whitehorse Press books are also available at
discounts in bulk quantity for sales and promotional
use. For details about special sales or for a catalog of
motorcycling books, videos, and gear write to the
publisher:
  Whitehorse Press
  107 East Conway Road
  Center Conway, New Hampshire 03813
  Phone: 603-356-6556 or 800-531-1133
  E-mail: CustomerService@WhitehorsePress.com
  Internet: www.WhitehorsePress.com

ISBN 1-884313-53-1

5 4 3 2 1

Printed in China

Acknowledgments

This book could not have been written without the help, advice, and support of my best friend, riding buddy, and wife, Sharon. Other important helpers include riding buddies: Tad Hetu, Mike Means, Eric Nelsen, and my brother, Roger.

Thanks, too, to the nice people at Whitehorse Press for the encouragement and advice.

Contents

Introduction

Imagine a twisting ocean-view highway speckled with secluded sandy beaches and pine scented mountain roads with ancient trees and volcano views. Picture high, rolling, golden hills, sharp, craggy canyons, ancient river-cut canyons showing all their geological secrets in their basalt sides. In your mind, project an image of a high purple desert with the sun rising on a straight, lonely highway leading to vast virgin forests. It's no wonder that bikers love to tour the Pacific Northwest.

Mild weather, beautiful and varied terrain, friendly people, great food, and tourist accommodations: this is a place to visit again and again. As a long-time resident of this motorcyclists' paradise, I consider most of these rides as my friends. These friends are sometime famous, somtimes secret—known only to us locals. There are lost roads which, like names dropped off a too-long Christmas card list, surface with warm familiarity when encountered by chance.

Mist clings to the ancient British Columbia forests on the way to Tofino.

My goal is to open the Pacific Northwest to outsiders who are looking for a memorable new ride and to reacquaint residents with some of their long-lost amigos. If you want more than an ordinary tour, this book is for you.

Motorcycle Journeys Through the Pacific Northwest is designed to give motorcyclists unforgettable routes in Oregon, Washington, and British Columbia. At 500,000 square miles, this is an area nearly half the size of the entire European Union. It would be easy to waste precious vacation time merely getting to a certain place, so we will focus on the journey and not the destination.

White waterfalls cascade down the walls of Stevens Pass in Washington.

How to Use this Book

I love desert rides, especially while dawn breaks over the sleeping land and the air smells fresh. Twisting mountain roads with tall dark forests and stunning views get my heart beating fast. Motoring peacefully along the coast with the vast and inspiring Pacific Ocean beside me fills me with a joy and peace that could not be understood by a non-biker. I just flat-out love to ride. My purpose is to give my reader a chance at some of these beautiful bike trips. It would be a shame to spend your time in the Pacific Northwest in hot, crowded places eating fast food and looking at billboards. This book will serve as a guide for both visitors and residents who want a great motorcycling experience. I offer my perception of the characteristics of the routes and leave it to my readers to decide what they would like to try. Not everyone likes to arise before dawn and ride the desert.

I've included directions that can be torn out of this book for placement in a tank bag window. The mileages should not be interpreted as exactly precise. Everyone rides differently. I often stop for photos and to gather other information, so my miles may be different from yours. When my notes conflicted with my maps and software, I've attempted to find the most accurate measurements. My distance notes should not be depended upon for precise fuel stops, but as a general idea of how how far things are apart.

The routes I suggest are merely starting points for adventure and discovery. You may discover your own secret roads, perfect vista, best apple pie, or friendliest inn.

You might wonder why most of these journeys begin from an urban hub. Since it's common for bikers to fly in and rent, many of these rides start from an urban area near available rentals. Most bike owners in the Pacific Northwest live in these urban hubs, also. If you are coming up from California or Nevada, west via Idaho, or south from Canada, you should notice that many of these routes are just right for the long-distance biker.

What This Book is Not

This book is not meant to take the place of a good set of maps or stopping someplace for directions when lost. Even as a local, I always travel with maps. I also don't pretend to know every great stop for photos and pie. Picture this book as a chat with a friendly traveler who's been down the road and is willing to point you in the right direction. I'd like to hear from you if you make a discovery not mentioned in this book or notice an error. Please write to me through my website www.mjpnw.com.

Sunset just south of Tolavanah, Oregon. These rocks punctuate the perfect, sandy Oregon beaches and allow a walker to adopt them for his own.

Rentals

As I said, travelers frequently fly in and rent bikes. Many beautiful Harleys, BMWs, and Hondas, as well as other bikes, are available to rent in the Pacific Northwest. Please note the contact numbers in the appendix, and book early if you want a certain bike.

Check with your insurance carrier to see what kind of protection your company allows you to take with you. Canadian police like to see that you have a Canadian insurance card; most companies provide these free if you request them.

I always advise renters to buy the insurance the rental company sells; otherwise a dump truck could run over your parked Harley and you pay $20,000. Some rental companies allow you to put other riders in your group on the rental agreement so you can switch bikes around. Some companies will meet you at the airport.

Many of these rental places will provide gear for free or low cost, but I suggest you bring your own helmet and riding clothes. If you are counting on the rental agency to provide gear, make sure you check with them ahead of time. Every Pacific Northwest state and province has a helmet law.

Gear/Weather/Climate/Riding Conditions

Keep in mind that your gear should be appropriate for the weather. Summers can be quite hot, even in the northern mountains and high eastern plateaus. Temperatures can also vary as much as 40 degrees from valley floor to mountain peak. Visitors should expect mostly dry, sunny weather during the summer, July and August being the driest months. My suggestion is to always wear armored clothing, boots, and gloves in addition to your helmet. Modern technology allows properly protected riders to be quite comfortable in all but the hottest weather. I nearly always keep a rain suit tucked in a bag.

Your bike should be in excellent touring condition with good tires, brakes, and fluids. Rentals are usually in tiptop shape. Some of the places you'll go will be far from the bike shop. Know the range of your bike and closely monitor fuel levels.

The Pacific Northwest is a huge place with coastal vistas, snow-capped mountains, vast deserts, soggy rain forests, and volcanic wastelands. Riding varies from narrow, twisting mountain roads to laser-beam-straight desert slabs. Some days a rider might easily put in 300 miles, others less than 100. With all this variation, it is truly a biker's paradise.

Maps and Directions

The maps included in this book are only intended to supplement good road maps. My suggestion is to orient your road map to the details in this book and use a highlighter to plan your trip. This would be especially important when navigating urban and congested valley corridors, where it's difficult to stop and figure out which freeway you want to be on.

Accommodations

After a hard 300-mile day, the idea of pitching a tent, even in a clean and sweet-scented campground, lacks appeal to me. I'd rather soak in a shower with a clean bed and mindless TV show waiting for me—perhaps a window air conditioner throbbing away to mask the snores of my sleeping brother. I like my bike parked just outside my motel room. My sweet wife likes to stay in romantic bed-and-breakfasts, so I will make suggestions about these when I have first-hand knowledge of them. The Pacific Northwest has plenty of clean, small, independent motels, as well as all the chains. Personally, I hate the Shilo Inn chain, but you may have a different experience than I have had.

I camp for a week or two each year so for travelers who like to remain connected with the outdoor experience all day and night, I will suggest campgrounds. The northwest has amazing campgrounds that can make a person feel intimately connected with nature.

Winter Reading

This book is also designed to be good reading on wet winter nights, not just a list of recipe-style directions. You will notice that some of these trips are described in a story format, while others speak more directly about the trip. I want you to take all these trips in your mind without ever getting your boots dusty.

In some areas of the Pacific Northwest you should be mindful of rocks or gravel in the road.

Checking Road and Traffic Conditions

Oregon
(800) 977-6368
www.tripcheck.com

Washington State Traffic Info
Dial 511 (just like 911, but not for emergencies) and say "traffic," then the
road number.
Also www.wsdot.wa.gov.

Canada
www.th.gov.bc.ca/bchighways/roadreports/roadreports.htm

Ferry Information

(206) 464-6400 (Seattle calling-area and out-of-state)
(888) 808-7977 (In-state)
(800) 843-3779 (Automated in-state information)

Port Angeles to Victoria
www.cohoferry.com

Black Ball Transport, Inc.
(360) 457-4491
(800) 833-6388 (TTY)

www.bcferries.bc.ca/schedules/

Washington State Parks

(888) 226-7688
www.parks.wa.gov

Weather in Canada

http://weatheroffice.ec.gc.ca/forecast/canada/bc_e.html

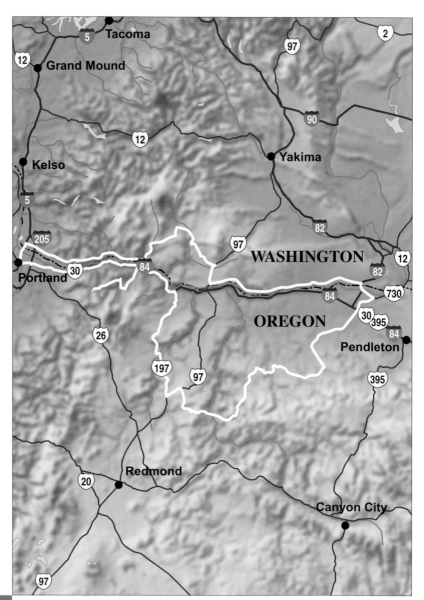

Oregon Treasures

Have you ever been alone in a strange house? Maybe you were a kid and your parents signed the papers on your new place. What did you do when you walked in? Did you notice that the house seemed to be quietly listening to find out who you were? Overcoming your shyness, you opened every drawer, door, and cubby. The house became yours.

A resting biker prepares to launch down the slab of Washington's US Highway 2 over Stevens Pass.

The great State of Oregon has registered thousands of motorcycles, yet few of these riders have ever experienced the finest rides near Portland. Since Portland is built around sweet, high rolling hills, many bikers seem comfortable only riding the curves near town.

This is like inspecting only one room in a new home. The Oregon Treasures chapters throw open secret doors that will forever remain concealed to uncurious locals or visitors to this area.

Trip 1 can be done in just two days, revealing hidden routes that will delight and excite even the most experienced local riders. Along the way, hundreds of mysterious highways tempt a rider to veer from the route to explore new secrets. These are the unopened doors in the new house. I say go for it.

Recently, I took the first part of this ride with my friend Tad and 400 other bikers from the Rose City Motorcycle Club (www.rose-city-mc.org). Tad and I had explored much of this route over the years, but to see it all-at-once proved to be a stunning experience for us. We couldn't quite wrap our minds around all that we beheld. After the ride, our photos seemed so absurdly small. We had to return.

Spring green grasses will give up their color when the sunny, dry summers gild the hills near John Day, Oregon.

Wheat fields take advantage of the fertile soil near Condon, Oregon.

On other rides with our friend, Eric and my brother, Roger, we discovered Oregon's big secret: Condon area roads. These roads are truly the finest biking roads in all the Pacific Northwest. This is one part of the house you must explore.

Tourists pour into the Hood River area each summer for the Columbia River wind surfing. The Hood River Fruit Loop will reveal to a biker why this area has had a long history of terrific motorcycling. When you ride on the Old Columbia River Highway (Highway 30 just south of The Dalles), you will appreciate the brilliance of engineer Sam Lancaster. During the 1920s, he designed the roads that grace the cover of this book and the basalt cliffs of the Columbia River Gorge.

Think about what's out there for you when you take these Oregon journeys: deep forest hallways, arid hill-hugging highways, wide desert chutes, antique brilliantly-engineered ribbons of asphalt cut into hard rock cliffs, great food, and friendly people. These rides are true Oregon Treasures.

Oregon is the huge house that belongs to you, the biker. Imagine you are alone in this great house. Don't be shy. No one will complain if you open every door and cupboard. Yield to your curiosity. The only way I know to truly sample Oregon's treasures is to try the rides in this section.

Trip 1 Lower Columbia Basin Sampler

Distance *575 miles (Two long days, or three if it's hot)*

Terrain *The best and most varied types of riding available in the entire Pacific Northwest: riverside highways, narrow rural byways, canyon side twisties, relaxed, arid, two-lane sweeping turns, perfect motorcycle roads near Condon, smooth sweeping turns running along gravel mountains, old, carefully-engineered historic highways, a few miles on blasting interstates. This is a long, demanding ride. Don't force yourself to keep going if the heat or other factors tire you. Watch for deer and rocks near cliff faces. Watch for tractors lingering around blind turns.*

Highlights *Columbia River Gorge, Mt. Adams, perfect biking roads near Condon, Stonehenge replica, Old Columbia River Highway, views of canyons, mountains, plains, and farms*

View from Rowena Viewpoint west of The Dalles. In 1922, Engineer Sam Lancaster built a curvaceous highway with a minimum width of 24 feet, grades no steeper than 5 percent, and no curve radii less than 100 feet. Whoopee!

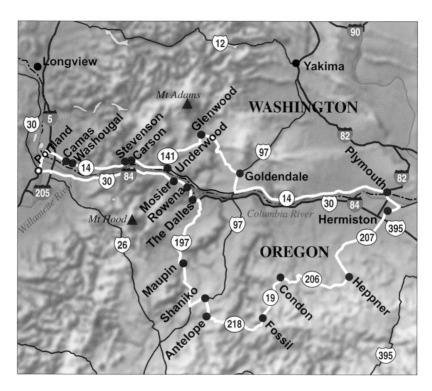

Sometimes you want to be first in line. Sometimes you want all the traffic lights to be green. Sometimes you just don't want to settle for something. You want the best. If you can take only one journey in the Pacific Northwest, the Lower Columbia Basin Ride is the green light, the front of the line, the best.

This journey takes you near an interesting volcano, **Mt. Adams,** up bare golden hills bridging the gap between the volcanic matter from Mt. Adams and the amazingly hard basalt slabs that make up most of the Columbia River Basin.

When you ride out of Portland, you are going to head directly for the Columbia River. This great body of water drains an area the size of France and is truly one of the world's prestigious rivers. To explore the whole river basin would take well over a week. I'm giving you this part of the basin in two days.

Begin this journey in **Portland, Oregon**—a hilly, handsome city built near the confluence of the **Willamette River** and the **Columbia River.** Head north toward **Seattle.** The two main freeways that will take you there are Interstate 5 (I-5) or Interstate 205. Once you cross the Columbia River, watch

The Route from Portland

Day 1

0   Leave Portland going north on Interstate 5 toward Seattle

9   Turn east onto Highway 14 toward Camas

61   Turn north onto 141 toward Trout Lake

69   Turn right toward Glenwood, follow signs

87   At Glenwood, follow signs to Goldendale

111 Turn right onto 142 toward Klickitat

134 At Lyle, turn east onto 14

162 At Hwy. 97 junction, explore Maryhill Museum and Stonehenge

169 Stay on 97 toward Goldendale. Two miles past Goldendale turn off for viewpoint. If it's clear, you can see four volcanoes. Turn around and go back to the Columbia River and Highway 14

184 Turn east onto 14

264 Turn south onto Interstate 82

277 Turn East toward Pendleton onto Interstate 84

281 Take exit to Highway 207 (Maybe stay in Heppner or Condon)

334 207 turns into 206. You want to be on 206 toward Condon

343 Arrive in Condon

Day 2

0   Leave Condon going south on 19 toward Fossil

21   At Fossil, go south onto 218 toward Antelope

57   Once in Antelope, go north to Shaniko

65   At Shaniko, turn south onto 97

77   Turn north onto 197

107 At Maupin, take a break in the park

142 Turn west on Highway 30 to The Dalles. Go through town staying on 30.

156 Enjoy the Rowena Look Out. Stay on 30 to Mosier.

167 At Mosier, get on Interstate 84 to head back to Portland

237 Arrive in Portland

for signs indicating Highway 14. Turn north on 14 toward **Camas** and **Washougal.** After passing through these two small towns, you will notice the suburban views becoming more rural. The river on your right, a mixed evergreen/deciduous forest on your left, and the gently winding roads tell you that you've truly begun this journey.

Stevenson rests comfortably just 30 miles from Camas. The town seemed to be dying until a big luxury resort, **Skamania Lodge,** was constructed just west of town. Now its short main street vibrates with life, its veins running rich with tourists' money. When taking this trip, I often stop for food at the **Wind River Inn** in **Carson** or the **River View Restaurant** in Stevenson. If I have guests, I'll pull into the Skamania Lodge for a terribly expensive breakfast.

From Stevenson, continue east on 14 to **Underwood.** Just past the **Klickitat River,** turn north onto Highway 141 toward **Trout Lake.** Continue on this road past pretty farms, woods, and ever-steeper rolling hills. At **B Z Corner,** barely a town, look for the signs to **Glenwood.** Turn right on B Z/Glenwood Road toward Glenwood. By now you will find that Mt. Adams has become close and perhaps even familiar. Mt. Adams is graced by a dozen glaciers and skirted round by miles of pristine forests and gentle farmland.

Looking north toward Washington from Rowena Viewpoint. The Columbia River Gorge can be perfect in April.

CHAPTER
1

Since northwesterners prize huckleberries, a small, tart blueberry-like fruit, pickers flock to this area in late summer to gather berries and hike the trails around Mt. Adams.

Once you leave Glenwood, you will be riding on a plateau toward **Goldendale**. All around you will be the high brown hills of this part of southern Washington. They go on forever and become more beautiful with each mile. You can't explore them on this trip. Instead, after about 24 miles on the Goldendale Highway, turn right on Highway 142 toward **Klickitat.**

The Klickitat River has cut a sinuous trail through the hard rock of the plateau. Bikers love the pretty views and twisting turns. Part of this highway is one lane, but it's all paved.

The Klickitat Hotel has blah food, but friendly people. Obey the local speed limits and continue down the highway to the Columbia River and Highway 14. Go east (left). When you get to the junction of Highway 97, turn left and follow the signs to the **Maryhill Museum.**

Besides being a stunning mansion looking out on beautiful views of the **Columbia River Gorge,** it has a nice lawn and shade. About two minutes from the museum is a full-sized replica of Stonehenge.

With your mind refreshed by Maryhill, turn your bike back to Highway 14 and go east. From here, 14 takes you along the edge of the Columbia River with the basalt cliffs on your left. You'll see few other travelers along this route, which is devoid of trees, but rich in geological beauty and golden-stemmed grasses.

When you eat here, you'll feel like you are in someone's friendly kitchen. Antelope Café was known as Zorba the Budda when the town was taken over by a religious cult in the '80s.

Just east of Glendale, the Glenwood-Goldendale Road snakes up high naked hills. The revealed apexes put smiles on biker's faces.

Your ride on 14 will end about 90 miles out of Goldendale, but if you love terrific motorcycle roads, the best is yet to come. When you get to Interstate 82, jump on this freeway going south toward **Hermiston.** After about 15 miles on I-82, you will need to merge onto I-84 going toward **Pendleton,** Oregon, for 3.5 miles, then take the Highway 207 exit going south (exit number 182).

This gets you to where you want to be: the best motorcycle roads in all the Columbia River Basin. Because of the great Missoula Flood, see Trip 6, this area features enormous piles of gravel atop basalt slabs. For bikers this means twisty roads.

Stay on 207 to **Heppner.** Visitors love Heppner for its unspoiled rural character. Have a picnic in the park or just rest on the grass. This pretty town was named after Harry Heppner, a mule freight operator who built a camp here at the confluence of three creeks. You want your mind clear for the ride between Heppner and **Condon.**

Many tourists who visit Heppner go for the fall bird hunting. If it's not hunting season, you can stay in one of the lodges like **Ruggs Ranch.** Otherwise check out the lodging recommendations at the end of this chapter.

Doesn't this view of the Glendale-Goldendale Road make your throttle hand itch?

From Heppner, though the road below you will not turn to gold, the gold will be in the turns. The roads are so great because of the combination of terrific scenery, quality pavement, and revealed apexes—few blind turns. Watch for deer, especially near dawn or dusk.

If you stay on 207, you'll notice it turns into 206 going toward Condon.

From Condon, you want to go south toward **Fossil** on Highway 19. Fossil was named for the fossil remains a rancher found on his property. Later, Thomas Condon found the fossilized bones of a saber-toothed tiger here.

At Fossil, head south onto Highway 218 toward **Antelope.** In Antelope, you can keep the magic going if you head north on 218 toward **Shaniko.** The Old West theme has taken over this tourist mecca. Make sure you tour their restored hotel.

At Shaniko, turn south on Highway 97 in order to tour the **Tygh Valley.** Twelve miles from Shaniko, turn north on Highway 197. This turn marks the end of the twisty rural roads, and the beginning of smooth, open, sweeping turns atop enormous smooth mountains of glacial and flood gravel deposits. One of these gravel mounds is several thousand feet high. Now that's gravel! The roads are beautifully paved and well banked.

You'll love the way 197 twists coming into **Maupin,** a major river-rafting center along the **Deschutes River.** The city park is great for a picnic or a shady nap in the grass. Leaving **Maupin,** you'll stay on 197 to see the grandest of the grand gravel hills—usually covered in golden wheat.

As you approach the town of **The Dalles,** make a left on Highway 30. This part of 30 will turn into the **Historic Columbia River Highway.** Stay on 30 toward Rowena. This will run you parallel to Interstate 84 and onto one of the most unreal stretches of highway to be found anywhere.

You've probably heard of the House of Mystery, where strange things happen, or The Vortex, where gravity and perspective go haywire. At the **Rowena Overlook,** you experience slow twisting roads where your floorboards never scrape. It's not magic; special engineering that took into consideration the underpowered automobiles of the 1920s made it possible. Rowena's panoramas of the Columbia River Gorge are among the best views of this whole trip. Don't miss this scenery.

Continue to follow Highway 30 as it winds down the hill to **Mosier.** From Mosier, take I-84 to Portland. From here, the only magic spell for me is the one woven by the knowledge that home is near, and I'll soon sleep in my own bed.

Winding along Highway 218 west of Fossil, Oregon, the roads reveal much to bikers.

CHAPTER
1

As you blast down I-84 toward Portland, you can look back at the wonders you experienced. I doubt if anyone could adequately explain the joys of this trip to someone who rides it on four wheels.

Mt. Adams, Stonehenge, the gorge, the perfect rural roads near Condon, the mammoth mounds after Maupin, the stunning roads and views of Rowena: how could strangers understand it all? Maybe if the person you spoke to had walked into a department store to use the restroom and was greeted by a big band, lights, and the owner saying, "Congratulations, you are our millionth customer!" That person might be able to imagine your feelings.

You got the best.

These curves near Condon can put a biker into a zone no one but us motorcyclists can understand.

CHAPTER

1

This rider emerges from a tight canyon to an open area just east of Antelope, Oregon.

Best Roads

You might wonder why I suggest you journey to Condon. Years ago, a group of friends and I set out to find the best biking roads in the Pacific Northwest. We traveled all over British Columbia, Washington, and Oregon. Our quest took us to Highway 19 from Sheep Rock Unit to Condon. The closer we came to Condon, the more spectacular the roads became. The four of us unanimously agreed that the roads around Condon are the best in the whole Pacific Northwest.

We defined a great road as possessing abundant, well-banked curves with a minimum of blind turns. We wanted reasonably high quality pavement with few potholes and bumps. The traffic should be minimal and predictable. Finally, the scenery should be such that we wouldn't mind traveling the route over and over again. The only negative for this route is the abundance of deer. When traveling this area in the morning or evening, we always see deer.

CHAPTER

1

Between Heppner and Condon, Oregon, this highway is one of the best motorcycling roads in the whole Pacific Northwest.

Heppner Food and Lodging

Ruggs Ranch
(541) 676-5390
(Reservations only after Sept. 1 due to hunting season)

Northwest Motel & RV Park
(541) 676-9167

Pizza in the bowling alley (Shamrock Lanes)

John's Other Place for family dining

Commuter Cafe for breakfast and lunch

Shaniko Food and Lodging

The Shaniko Historic Hotel
(541) 489-3441
(800) 483-3441

Renting Bikes In Oregon

In Oregon, only Harleys are available for rent. This is largely due to the prohibitive liability insurance rates. Since Harley is self-insured, the bikes tend to be new and in perfect condition. Washington State and British Columbia offer more bike choices.

A visitor can rent Harleys from two different places in the Portland area: Latus Motors and Paradise Harley. Latus is closer to the airport, but Paradise Harley will shuttle you to your bike if you make prior arrangements. A renter must be 21 (or 25 — check web sites) years old or older, possess a valid motorcycle license, and have proper motorcycle gear (DOT approved helmet). Some places, like AMC in Albany, will provide you with a helmet and raingear as part of your rental. AMC also has great rates.

If you want to take a tank bag, make sure it's in great condition. These dealers are very sensitive about scratches on their bikes.

I suggest you buy the collision damage wavier, but you can check with your insurance or credit card company to see if they cover this for you. If a Humvee totals your bike while you are in getting a sandwich, you suddenly own $20,000 worth of junk. Call, or visit the websites to get more information.

Latus Motors 870 E Berkeley St. Gladstone, OR 97027 (503) 249-8653 www.latus-hd.com

Paradise Harley 10770 SW Cascade Ave. Tigard, OR 97223 (503) 924-3700 www.paradiseh-d.com

American Motorcycle Classics 1600 Century Drive NE Albany, OR 97322 (503) 928-6234 www.amchd.com

Condon Food and Lodging

Condon Motel
(541) 384-2181

Hotel Condon
(800) 201-6706
www.hotelcondon.com

Café Condon
(541) 384-7000

Trip 2 Hood River Fruit Loop

Distance *150 miles (I suggest you spend a day in Hood River Valley and a night in the town of Hood River)*

Terrain *Once in the Hood River Valley, nearly every road is a pleasant rural highway or a charming, narrow forest road. Roads tend to be in good condition, but watch out for tourist traffic on weekends, animals—especially in morning and afternoon—forest debris, and rare gravel patches on some forest roads.*

Highlights *Charming rural highways, twisting, deep forest roads, unbelievable views of Mt. Hood and the Oregon fruit tree industry. Lost Lake offers perfect picnicking and photo ops. During spring and fall, this route is called the Fruit Loop.*

With her back turned to Mt. Hood, and her face toward Mt. Adams, this biker admires the views in Hood River Valley.

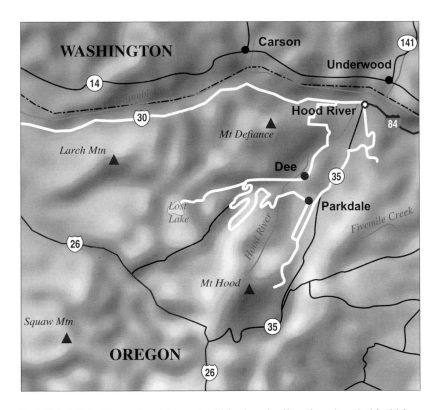

In 1924, Wells Bennett, with most of his daredevil racing days behind him, roared up **Mt. Hood** to the 8,500-foot elevation on his four-cylinder Henderson. A group on foot started out on the same July 4th morning and easily out-paced him due to the abundance of piano-sized boulders that constantly presented themselves in front of him. Although eager to reach the summit, after four days of scrambling, he was finally defeated by a stinging snowstorm and blinding winds. No one has ever made it higher on a motorcycle.

This journey is told from the point of view of a traveler coming from **Portland** since most visitors approach the Hood River area from Portland by driving through the **Columbia River Gorge**—a dream of a journey. Local bikers like to make any excuse to take the **Columbia River Scenic Highway** (Highway 30) when in the gorge, but sometimes we are in a hurry.

For the most direct route, you turn off Interstate 84 on Exit 64 going toward State Highway 35. Morning is the best time for this trip due to the high winds that usually pick up during the afternoon. The trip can be exhausting when the gorge winds are at 50 mph.

CHAPTER

1

The Route From Portland

0   Leave Portland going east on Interstate 84 toward The Dalles

65   Exit I-84 toward Highway 35 (Mt. Hood)

67   Look for the sign toward Panorama Point on the right side of the road. Turn left and follow signs to Panorama Point.

72   Leave Panorama Point and continue south on Eastside Road

75   Turn left onto Wells Drive

76.5   Turn left onto Fir Mountain Road and go until the pavement ends

79   Backtrack past Wells Drive. Fir Mountain Road will veer west toward Highway 35

89   Turn left (south) onto Highway 35

95   Turn right onto Cooper Spur Road toward Parkdale. Stay on Cooper Spur Road. There are some excellent twisties. Watch for possible gravel in spots.

100.8   This is Cooper Spur Inn. To ride the Lost Lake tour, retrace your route to Parkdale.

106.9   From Parkdale, follow the signs to Lost Lake. I'll give you directions, but I suggest you just follow the signs. There are plenty of them and the road is so pretty. Left onto Baseline.

107.5   Right onto Old Parkdale Road

108.6   Left onto National Forest Road 16 (Red Hill Road).

112   Right on Tony Creek Road

112.5   Sharp left onto Carson Hill Road (this will become Lost Lake Road)

119.6   Stay on Lost Lake Road

125.1   Arrival at Lost Lake. From Lost Lake to Hood River, take Lost Lake Road toward Dee.

145.9   Lost Lake Road becomes Dee Highway (Hood River Highway). This will take you right into Hood River.

More spectacular than a mountain, viewing the apple trees can trigger a need to return in the fall for terrific apples and other fruit.

In a grocery store you can find about five or six varieties of apples. Come to Hood River to see and taste 20 or more apple and pear varieties.

CHAPTER
1

After leaving the interstate, stay on the route toward Highway 35. About a mile from the exit, and just after the last stop sign, look for the turn on your left toward **Panorama Point.** Some maps designate this as Panorama Point Road and others show it as East Side Road. Don't feel bad if you miss this turn. There's no pull-out lane and you may have traffic behind you. It seems I miss it about 50 percent of the time. It's worth backtracking to see the view. Snaking up to the **Panorama Point Park,** you will be teased by twisty little roads spidering off here and there. Most of these end in gravel, but I still enjoy exploring them.

If you can manage to visit Panorama Point in the morning, you are in for a fantastic view of Mt. Hood and the apple tree-filled valley before it. In the afternoon, the view becomes back-lit and not as nice for photos. After pictures and using the restroom, continue south on East Side Road. After a couple of miles, follow Wells Drive to Fir Mountain Road. This narrow road takes you past glorious views of Mt. Hood until the pavement ends. How I long to have

Bikers charge up the Old Columbia River Highway west of The Dalles.

Parts of the Old Columbia River Highway run through woods with picnic areas and waterfall hikes sprinkled throughout.

a good gravel bike at this point! Instead, I turn around, retracing my route for a mile until I can turn left on Ehrck Hill Road. Take Ehrck Hill Road to 35. Turn left.

Highway 35 will take you past miles of apple and pear trees. In the spring the blossoms draw thousands of tourists. Motorcyclists get to smell the fragrance. In the fall, the air is sweet with the heavy sugary smell of apples and pears. We never buy enough. They taste so good, and an apple shopper can go far beyond the five varieties carried by most supermarkets. Stop, sample, and buy apples if they are available.

About six miles from Ehrck Hill Road, you will see the **Cooper Spur** turn off. Follow this to the **Cooper Spur Ski Area.** When you go through the tiny berg of **Mount Hood**, look for the house just north of the big beautiful barn. That is the former home of Wells Bennett, the famous motorcyclist, who would race his 40-horsepower Henderson against early airplanes and anything else that was fast.

For a couple of miles after the village of Mount Hood, you will be amongst row after row of fruit trees. As they end, the road becomes sinuous, with intermittent potholes and thickening fir trees as you gain altitude. Occasional picturesque ranches backed by high rounded hills appear along the way.

Travelers enjoy the beautifully restored Hood River Hotel for its food and atmosphere.

At the top, just after a set of glorious twisties, you can find a restaurant and clean guest cottages at the **Inn at Cooper Spur.** If you want to brave the gravel roads of the area, you can get to the **Cloud Cap Inn.**

My bike is strictly for the pavement, so about a half-mile from the ski area, I can take a wooded road east to connect to 35 if I want to blast out of the **Hood River Valley,** but if I have the time, I like to head north to the lazy, heavily-wooded roads leading to **Lost Lake** and its terrific lake/mountain views.

This is going to sound complicated. If you want, toss the book into the tank bag and just follow the signs to **Packwood,** then to Lost Lake. If you like directions, here goes.

To get to Lost Lake, retrace your way down the Cooper Spur Road for four miles until you can turn left at Evans Creek Road. After a half-mile, turn right on Clear Creek Road and run into the little artsy town of **Parkdale.** Besides art, the two main industries are packing apples and providing nice homes for retirees. From here the fastest way to get to Lost Lake is to proceed the 3.5 miles to the town of **Dee** and follow the signs to Lost Lake Road.

Mt. Hood shines in a summer morning. View from Fir Mountain Road on the east side of Hood River Valley.

Try to imagine the clean, pine smell along this road to Lost Lake.

If you love to spend time on lonely deep-forest roads, at Parkdale, turn left at Red Hill Drive and follow it for a quarter-mile until it becomes County Road 16. Stay on this twisty, narrow county road for about 15 miles until you come to County Road 18. Stay on this for two miles. You get to cross the West Fork of Hood River just less than a mile before County Road 13. What a view! Turn left on County Road 13 and enjoy it for five miles.

These directions may appear difficult, but few people have ever gotten lost watching for the plentiful signs pointing the way to Lost Lake. Once you are at Lost Lake, you can get snack foods at their little market, have a picnic with a perfect view of lake and mountain, take the spongy fern trail around the lake, rent a boat or canoe (no power boats allowed) and fish, swim in the clear waters, and take a camp site for the night (reservations recommended). Once while eating sandwiches in the picnic area, we watched a daddy and his young son catch a 20-inch rainbow trout from a rented rowboat.

Indian legends hold Lost Lake as a place of bad luck. It is told that at a great gathering on the lake, a host of Indians were about to enjoy a feast when a snow-white doe, pursued by wolves, jumped into the clear waters. It swam out to the middle, dived beneath the surface and was never seen again. The medicine man judged this to be an omen of bad luck. The whole group left immediately.

When you leave this lake, follow the Lost Lake Road toward **Dee,** not really a town, more a location on a map. Driving though this area, I could never figure out why it has a name. Once on the Dee Highway, follow the signs toward Hood River.

If you want romance, try the **Hood River Hotel,** a pretty, restored hotel in the center of the charming town of **Hood River.** If you want elegance and cost is no object, the **Columbia Gorge Hotel** offers stunning luxury to soothe tired bones. Affordable, clean lodging can be found at the **Comfort Suites.** Get breakfast at **Bette's Place** or a gourmet dinner at **Brian's Pourhouse.**

The well-maintained buildings of Hood River might charm you or transport you back to the era of Wells Bennett and the barnstorming days of the twenties. A day in the Hood River Valley is a day surrounded by rustic and geological beauty.

Hood River Food and Lodging

Hood River Hotel & Pasquale's Ristorante
(800) 386-1859
www.hoodriverhotel.com

Best Western Hood River Inn
(800) 828-7873
www.hoodriverinn.com

Columbia Gorge Hotel
(541) 386-5566
www.columbiagorgehotel.com

Cooper Spur Mountain Resort
(541) 352-6692
www.cooperspur.com

Bette's Place
(541) 386-1880

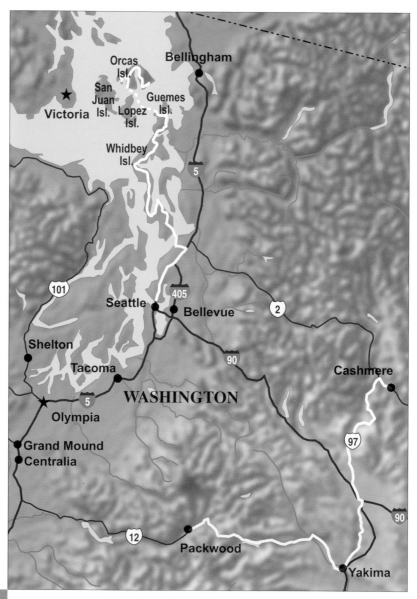

Evergreen State Rides

It's called the Evergreen State, but it possesses so many climates and attractions, that there are Washington State rides in nearly every section of this book.

When you think of The Evergreen State, don't images of perfect forests and the shinning Space Needle city of Seattle come to mind? In this section, a motorcycle traveler learns about peaceful, romantic islands that seem perfectly formed for bikers.

We step through a time portal to see some of the geological wonders of Central Washington—some taking millions of years to construct. We also visit the historical buildings of **Coupeville,** dressed and rouged like beautiful women just past their prime. We also get to step back to the 1950s on **Orcas Island** where fast food means smoked oysters, neighbors know each other, and the children all seem carefully nurtured.

Don't be fooled. Some of these soft brown hills have hard basalt cores. Others are mere piles of flood gravel.

Bikes line up just 15 miles from Cashmere so the riders can view the Columbia River.

These rides are amongst the slowest and easiest in this book. No high mileage days are possible or desirable when island hopping. For this reason, I suggest you consider these rides if introducing your honey to the joys of motorcycle travel. Here she can see the sights from a bike traveling at under 55 for most of the trip. Shops, sights, and little hikes abound so that you can make a good impression. You might think that these islands, floating in the moist Puget Sound, immerse a rider in precipitation as well as romance. Not true. Well, the romance can be there always, but the climates are surprisingly dry due to the Olympic Mountains. They soak up most of the moisture before it can get to the San Juan Islands.

Maybe I'm just too fond of seafood, but the restaurants in **Langley** and **East Sound** serve terrific food. Not only that, a biker can get a pretty bed and breakfast overlooking the water, a bottle of wine, and some fresh seafood from the markets to make a world class meal right in your own place. Touring the San Juan Islands is more like a cruise ship experience—slow and relaxing.

Making the run from Packwood to Cashmere is more like the Pacific Northwest outdoor-rough-it experience. Unlike the easy, slow days on the islands, this ride can be gritty, hot, and windy.

The ride from Packwood to Cashmere involves no island travel, but the stretch over the shoulders of **Mt. Rainier,** the ride along the **Yakima River** and finally rolling into **Leavenworth** are some of my favorite places in all the Pacific Northwest to ride. This ride involves some interstate highway travel and possible harsh midday and afternoon heat. I love the interplay of desert rock and pure blue river sandwiched between two deeply wooded areas of the state.

Cashmere and Packwood embody the perfect hubs from which to see many of the wonders of the Pacific Northwest. From Packwood, rides spider out to Mt. St. Helens, Mt. Rainier, and other journeys mentioned in this book. Cashmere is the launching pad for a ride west to Seattle, north to the Northern Cascades and Canada, or south along the mighty Columbia to all the treasures in Oregon. Terrific motorcycle roads connect these two small towns.

This is the true Evergreen State: the woods, desert, and rivers of Packwood to Cashmere, and the slow romantic, salt-air beauty of the San Juan Islands.

On a break from working on touring bike research, motorcycle journalist Tad Hetu stops at the Columbia River.

Trip 3   Seattle Area Getaway

Whidbey Island: From Mukilteo to Anacortes

Distance *69 miles (Three hours with few stops and fast ferries. I suggest lingering a day or two. Put a couple of hundred miles on your odometer.)*

Terrain *Lazy curves, no speed limits above 55, mostly 45 to 50, speed limits strictly enforced, principle hazards are deer and bicyclists*

Highlights *Island frame of mind and quiet, pleasant roads. Great food, quaint towns and farms. Views of dynamic currents, rocky shores, lakes, and placid waters of Puget Sound. Only 40 minutes north of Seattle.*

The vast green waters of Puget Sound flow deep and strong toward the narrow opening to Skagit Bay. View from northern tip of Whidbey Island.

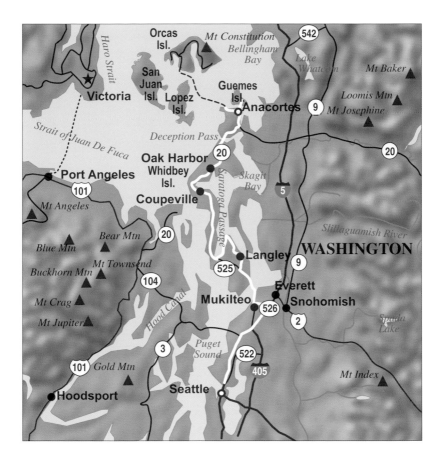

Have you ever felt a sense of pride that you were able to endure long distances on your bike with bad food, harsh weather, and terrible traffic? Softies in their cars would never last. Only a rider with tightly wound nerves of steel can travel in such conditions. This journey, however, is about pleasure, not endurance. It's about lazy, low mileage days with lots of stops in pretty places, great food, and mild weather. It's about pure enjoyment and relaxation. Nearly any biker can do this ride. I'm guessing all bikers will love **Whidbey Island.**

To get to this island from **Seattle**, you will need to take rides on the **Washington State Ferry** system (see sidebar on page 52). This can be hell in the summer if you have a car. That means you need to arrive hours before your ferry departs. Once we spent the night in our car on the ferry dock to make sure we caught our morning departure. With a motorcycle, it's different. Bikes go to the front of the line.

Double Bluff Beach on South Whidbey, just south of Freeland, is famous for its warm shallow waters, world class beach combing, and the amazing 400 foot high sandy bluff.

WARNING KEEP OFF
BLUFF IS PRIVATE PROPERTY
AND
EXTREMELY HAZARDOUS

Do you know what it feels like to ride past miles of cars waiting for a boat, go right to the ticket booth, and pay half price for your ticket? That feeling alone makes this trip a must.

The moment your bike touches the shore of the island, the relaxation factor oozes through your body. Unaware that they were tight, you feel your jaw muscles relax. A peaceful, pleasant feeling pushes away troubles and worries. The sea smell. The intense forest greens. The fresh air. Your heartbeat slows. It's an island frame of mind.

So often motorcycle touring is gritty and tense. I love it. But touring this place is different. With speed limits mostly around 40 and 50 mph, you never get to the tense part. Surrounded by pristine seas, sweet, dark forests, and easygoing farm lands, the gritty parts are left behind on the mainland. This is all about a relaxing and slow tour on winding, twisting roads. You want to avoid going fast due to the deer, bicyclists, and friendly police.

To start this journey, travel north from Seattle on Interstate 5. Take the Mukilteo/Highway 526 exit. Once in **Mukilteo,** you take the ferry to Whidbey Island. Exit the ferry and head up Highway 525. After 3.5 miles, take the turn toward **Langley.** Only two miles later you can park your bike and browse this tiny artists' town on the shores of **Saratoga Passage.** Langley has excellent restaurants, including **The Langley Café, The Fish Bowl,** and **The Star Bistro. The Dog House** has great fish and chips and clam chowder. During the summer you will likely need reservations at the first three restaurants and nearly anywhere you want to spend the night.

When my wife and I stay in Langley, we like **The Eagle's Nest Bed and Breakfast.** The clean rooms offer romance, art, and forest or sea views. The gourmet breakfasts are light but elegant. If you want to spend more, book a stay at **The Inn at Langley. The Langley Motel** prides itself on being no frills. There is also camping at the fairgrounds or **South Whidbey State Park.**

Langley does not have a lock on romance. The town of **Coupeville** is the second oldest in the state of Washington, with over 100 buildings listed in the National Historic Register. There's a whale skeleton, great ice cream, and strolling or cruising the shops and Victorian buildings. The waters of **Penn Cove** produce superb mussels, which are widely available throughout the island. **Toby's Tavern** sells mussels and other seafood delights. It can be a bit smoky. I like the soup, sandwich, and pie at **Kneed and Feed,** where you can watch the sea gulls drop clams onto the rocky beach then swoop down to pick the meat from the shattered shell.

This Coupeville tavern has great seafood and sandwiches. Spend time exploring this historic town.

CHAPTER
2

Standing on Whidbey Island and looking north, you see Fidalgo Island.

Whidbey Islanders are proud of their big island. At 50 twisting miles, it's the longest in the lower 48. Besides eating the great food, a visitor can take a pretty hike on a bluff trail at **Ebey State Park,** explore 300,000 years of geological history at **Double Bluff** beach access, or photograph this interesting island. Artists' shops and galleries abound. Get off the bike and enjoy the island.

A naval air base impacts the northern part of the island. The town of **Oak Harbor** has more fast food stands per capita than any other place in America. After the quaintness of South Whidbey, the harsh cacophony of backlit signs, slow traffic, and strip malls stand out in stark contrast. You might find your jaw muscles tightening as you sit at a stoplight. Still, Oak Harbor has nearly any service you might need, and you must pass through it to get to **Deception Pass.**

Did anyone ever tell you that the tidal difference between the Pacific and Atlantic Oceans is 19 feet at the Panama Canal? Have you wondered what would happen if the canal were at sea level with all locks open? Pretty violent currents right? You can see violent currents like this at Deception Pass. Only 200 yards at its narrowest point between Whidbey and **Fidalgo Island,** the mighty flood can actually throw a small boat back as it attempts to proceed between the **Strait of Juan de Fuca** and **Skagit Bay.**

Locals like to claim that more visitors come to **Deception Pass State Park** than the Grand Canyon. Why do all those people come? It could be the view of the wild currents 186 feet below the **Deception Pass Bridge.** It might be the camping, fishing, boating, and other recreational activities. Perhaps it's the wildlife, forests, and the 251 campsites.

You will be on State Route 20 as you approach the park. If you stop at the parking lot just before the bridge, it will cost you $5 in parking fees. You will get good restrooms and views from the south. If you cross the bridge and park in one of the turnouts, it is free, and you can still walk across the bridge to the bathrooms. Have your camera ready, and be prepared to gawk at the power below you.

Mukilteo, Washington has its pretty lighthouse standing guard over the ferry traffic. (Photo by Sharon Hansen)

CHAPTER

2

Langley, on South Whidbey Island, boasts terrific public art as well as great food.

I'm going to let you in on a secret that even many locals don't know about: **Mt. Erie.** The two-mile, paved road to the top of this 1,300-foot rock is worth the side trip. Since it's mostly one lane, you need to imagine an SUV coming down the road around each blind turn. Keep your speed down and your expectations for great views up.

To get to this pretty spot, continue north on State Highway 20 as you leave Deception Pass. After a mile or so you will see plenty of signs for **Lake Campbell.** As soon as you pass Lake Campbell, look for a road off to your left called Lake Campbell Road. Turn left on Lake Campbell Road. Take the next right at Lake Campbell Store. It's called Roy Ault Road. Continue on this for a mile until you see the signs for **Mount Erie Park.** All this while you will be twisting your neck to look at the huge rock you will be climbing to view Cascade and Olympic Mountains, as well as the **Skagit Valley** and dozens of islands floating in the mists.

From the park, just continue north to the town of **Anacortes.** Work your way to the downtown area and continue north. You will catch glimpses of **Fidalgo Bay** on your right, but that's not where you want to go. You want to go to 12th Street and turn left (west) toward the ferry dock.

This journey can be over in just a few hours, but oh how sweet it is to linger, try the terrific food, sample the cultural flavor of the little towns, and stroll the beaches looking for treasures. Take this ride with your honey and enjoy the romance. If time permits, link this trip to the Orcas Island Ride (Trip 4).

Langley Food and Lodging

Café Langley
(360) 221-3090
www.langley-wa.com/cl/

The Fish Bowl
(360) 221-6511
www.fishbowlrestaurant.com

Star Bistro Café & Bar
(360) 221-2627
www.star-bistro.com/

The Dog House
(360) 221-9996

Some of the Washington State Ferries have big cafeterias, but I favor taking a picnic on board. They all have good coffee.

CHAPTER
2

Using the Washington State Ferry System

Some residents of these islands use motorcycles, not for the joy of the sport, but just to take advantage of the ferry system. Many visitors tow their bikes to Mukilteo ($8 a day to park at the ferry dock), travel the islands, then tow their bikes back home. Here's how to do it:

1) Check the ferry schedule to see when your target ferry runs. Call (888) 808-7977 or visit www.wsdot.wa.gov/ferries.

2) Plan to arrive at the ferry dock at least 30 minutes before departure. You may pass several miles of waiting cars on your way to the dock. Pull up next to a toll kiosk. Dismount your bike and approach the window.

3) Pay your toll with credit card or cash, and receive instructions as to which of the numbered lines is for your ferry. Go to the front of that line and chat with the other bikers or go to the waiting room to read and wait for your ferry to be called. When your ferry is called, hustle out to your bike. You will be expected to board instantly, after the walkers and bicyclists.

4) A ferry employee will signal you to pull onto the ferry. As you drive into the dark metal throat of the ferry, you may notice the metal decks are wet. The ferry workers I talked to said they'd never seen anyone drop their bike on a wet deck—except for a rented Harley, when the rider forgot to deploy the kickstand.

When you think of crossing salt water, you think of waves and perhaps seasickness. Crossing the still waters of the Sound is different. Your bike will be just fine on its kickstand. Some ferries provide chalks to slide under your bike opposite from the kickstand.

5) During the ride you can go upstairs and eat a picnic meal (if you brought it with you), read, or nap on one of the 7-foot bench seats. Longer ferry routes have snack bars and even cafeterias. Check your route so you know exactly where you want to go once the ferry docks. When traffic is gushing off the ferry, you won't have time to check this. Keep track of the time. Once the speaker announces it's time for drivers to return to their vehicles, bikers need to make haste—you are first off after the walkers are clear.

6) Once the ferry is docked, you will be signaled to leave. Avoid revving your engine if you have loud pipes. It irritates the workers, who generally are very biker-friendly.

Langley Chamber of Commerce
www.whidbey.com/langley/

Langley Motel
(866) 276-8292
www.langleymotel.com
(Kitchen—no frills)

Inn at Langley
(360) 221-3033 (Reservations)
www.innatlangley.com
(Swanky)

Eagles Nest Inn
(360) 221-5331
www.eaglesnestinn.com
(Clean, pretty, artsy, friendly)

Coupeville Chamber of Commerce
www.centralwhidbeychamber.com

Camping on Whidbey Island

Deception Pass State Park
State parks pass or fee.

Ducken Road
Off Highway 20. Offers privately operated camping and RV parks. Fee.

Fort Ebey State Park
Many tent sites. State parks pass or fee.

Rhododendron County Park
Eight rustic campsites. No fee. Five-day limit.

South Whidbey State Park
Numerous tent and RV campsites. Large group site available by reservation.
State parks pass or fee.

Island County Fairgrounds in Langley
Tent and RV campsites, in-town location. Some electrical hookups. Fee.

Trip 4 Orcas Island Affair

Distance *200 miles (I suggest two days, one night)*

Terrain *Some congestion around the ferry dock and in the little tourist town of East Sound. Very tight turns on the road up to Mt. Constitution. Otherwise, mostly gentle sweeping turns. Watch for bikes and deer.*

Highlights *Island sights, smells, and the feeling of being away from it all. Views from Mt. Constitution. Rural sights seem from another era.*

This view of Summit Lake and Puget Sound from Mt. Constitution is the highest point on the San Juan Islands.

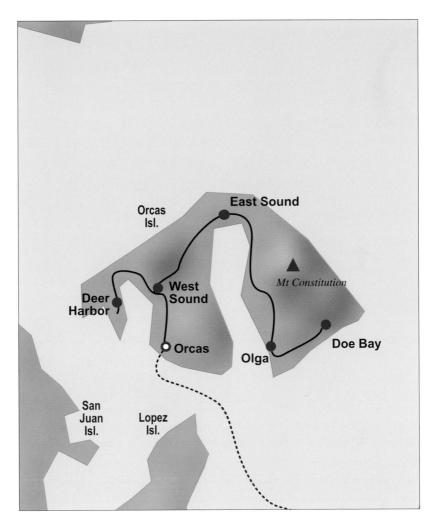

This island is so small, you can afford (and may perhaps desire) to make wrong turns. Keep in mind that when you leave the ferry and land on the island, turn left.

The story began when a pretty girl in a ponytail innocently took my hand and kissed it. It was inconceivable that such a perfect girl liked me. She was so fabulous, and I was just ordinary. We fell in love, raised two beautiful daughters, and had our first summer trip with no kids. Where to go? The story took us to **Orcas Island**—a place that brought all those ponytail feelings back to us. Of all the places I've biked, this is the one that holds the most sweetness and romance.

CHAPTER

2

The tight turns on the way to the top of Mt. Constitution can be real peg scrapers. (Photo by Sharon Hansen)

In my early life, I rode with no shirt, long hair down my back, and her arms around my waist. Our picnic was in a backpack. Of course now we ride in full armored clothing, short hair neatly in a helmet, picnic in the Givi top case, but just to be a bit wild, we leave our face shields open. She still holds on to me. I love it.

An ironbutt jockey might laugh at Orcas Island. No speed limits over 50. Bicyclists around each bend. The whole island is awash with semi-tame deer. This is not a place to attempt any blind turns with the bike tipped at a 40-degree angle. It is a place to smell the sea air, view rocky shores alive with hunting birds and shore life, and feel your honey's arms around your waist. Slow speeds allow a measure of conversation even without electronics. How romantic!

As soon as our ferry docked, bicyclists and walk-ons left the ship. We stopped our conversations with other traveling motorcyclists. Ferry traffic directors signaled us bikers. We charged up the ramp and another traffic worker aimed us to the left. Turns out, that was the right way. Sharon had booked us into a bed and breakfast. It had views of the sea and was not far from the dock. Then again, nothing on Orcas Island is very far from any place but our ordinary life.

CHAPTER

2

You know how everything looks different from the saddle of a bike? You can't explain to strangers how smells, colors, scenery, and even feelings seem more vivid from a saddle. The moment our tires touched the shore, the sea smells and blue skies surrounded us. It was like a "ferry" land.

In the next instant, we were in a forest tunnel on a sweet winding road. All the roads on Orcas are winding. They wind through forests, pretty farms, quaint villages, and along the rocky coast. They wind past the yellowy reds of the madrone tree with its waxy leaves. Bikers should like seeing madrone trees; they only grow in dry climates. Orcas Island usually has great weather.

The islanders work hard to make Orcas seem like something out of the 1950s. I didn't see any backlit signs or franchise restaurants or hotels. Everything looks neat but homemade. The kids look like someone just gave them a wash and a hug. People smile, leave their doors unlocked, and stop to ask if you need any help if you've pulled off to take a picture.

This stone observation tower, built by the Civilian Conservation Corps in the 1930s, offers views of Orcas and other San Juan Islands.

CHAPTER

2

These bikes went to the front of the ferry line to await transportation to various other islands. Behind them, the car line snakes endlessly back.

The photogenic qualities of this island kept calling us to stop and take another picture. Sharon phoned our bed and breakfast to say we were running late. She had booked this romantic place based on internet photos. It did not disappoint. Hidden in the woods, **Anchorage Inn** has four sea-facing units with mini kitchens, candles, soft music, and complimentary wine. There's a grill on the lawn that would see some fresh halibut later. The clothes-optional hot tub sits alone behind shrubs and trees and looks out at East Sound. The Inn's only drawback was a steep gravel drive that caused my heavy cruiser to slide nervously the first time we tried it. Go slow down the hill.

Islanders say there are four winds, but I like to think of this island as four rides. The first one involves packing your honey and a picnic then twisting up to the top of **Mount Constitution**—the highest point (2,400 feet) on all the San Juan Islands. The hairpin turns on the highway to the top are peg scrapers. The ever-present bicyclists will serve as reminders to go slow. Some of the turns are truly witchy.

You need to pay the $5 parking fee, but after you see the view, you'll think of this as one of the best bargains on the island. A stone observation tower dominates the peak and reveals the green and pewter mosaic of islands and mountains. This may be one of the most stunning panoramas in the Pacific Northwest.

Try one of the hiking trails from the top. They are engineering marvels constructed by the Civilian Conservation Corps in the 1930s. The power of harnessing the eager engine of jobless Americans radiates from this mountain to the pulse of ancient forests and the pull of silvery waters, dark green islands floating in mists, with snow-mantled mountains quietly watching over it all. Sharon slipped her hand into mine at a lookout spot. We felt alone in this living fantasy place.

Coming down from this mountain, we enjoyed exploring **Moran State Park.** Many bikers camp here for only $16 a night. The sites were generous, heavily wooded, and close to the shores of **Cascade Lake.** Swimming, boating (rentals), fishing, bird watching, and hiking: Moran State Park has all this and more than 130 campsites. Reserve these by calling (888) 226-7688 or visit www.parks.wa.gov.

The second ride can be a continuation of the Mount Constitution spin. Just keep going on Olga Road. Turn left at **Café Olga** (best cinnamon rolls on the island) toward **Doe.** Stay on this road to see coastal and farm views. Watch the horses graze. Smell the sea breezes. Shortly after the fire station, the road turns right and becomes Cow Hill Road. The pavement peters out after a mile. It made me wish I brought a better gravel bike.

The ride along Mountain Lake on Orcas Island refreshes the mind. (Photo by Sharon Hansen)

That night we sat out on our deck eating a salad covered in dungess crab meat and a slab of freshly barbecued halibut with a bottle of local wine. The sun cast horizontal beams onto the park across the sound. We had kayaks reserved for the morning. Ride three would include a paddle.

To get to **Deer Harbor** we headed toward **West Sound** and stayed on the coast-hugging road. Once you get to Deer Harbor, you'll notice there is no place to park. Our kayak company told us to park behind the post office. What a surprise! There are several secret parking spots there. Don't tell anyone about them.

There are more than half a dozen places to rent kayaks or book tours, but we chose **Shear Water Sea Kayak Tours.** Our guide, Jake, took us out to tour the **Wasp Islands.** We saw eagles, harbor seals, and other wildlife. One eagle boldly watched us as we quietly paddled close enough to see his cold amber eyes.

You don't need to get a guide to kayak around Orcas, but you need to know what you're doing. There are winds and currents that can cause a visitor problems. The waters are still with the exception of boat wakes and wind-blown chop.

Orcas Island farmers still work to the rhythm of the seasons.

Funny that Orcas Island people label a road scenic. Everything there is scenic. (Photo by Sharon Hansen)

To finish ride three, we took our bike to the end of Deer Harbor Road and enjoyed the hay smell of the pretty farms and the salt breezes. I thought about coming back to this island with friends. We could stay at the **Landmark Hotel** or camp. It would be a great trip, but not as romantic as with Sharon.

The next morning, our last on Orcas Island, we decided to have a lazy breakfast and ride the Enchanted Forest Road from **East Village** to **West Beach Resort** and take the Crow Valley Road back to the ferry dock. Standing in a mom and pop pottery store, I found myself wondering what enormous pottery thing Sharon was going to buy and how I was going to carry it back home. Every nook and cranny of our bike was packed. I was looking at some tiny blue salt and pepper shakers and saying how great they were, when I felt her hand in mine. An unexpected ponytail thrill fired through me. She still likes me. This Orcas Island story needs repeating.

CHAPTER

2

Trip 5 Packwood to Cashmere Run

Distance   *170 miles one way (all day with rest, photo, and gawking stops)*

Terrain   *About two-thirds rural highways, some quite twisty; the other third is two- and four-lane mountain/desert arteries*

Highlights   *Mountain views, deep forests, cliff-hugging rural highways, rapid climate changes from temperate rainforests to desert sage brush, geological wonders*

Remember Noah? First there was the flood. Washington state slept under the sea. As the Tectonic plates lifted the Evergreen State out of the waters, the area was flooded with basalt lava the thickness of cold pancake syrup. Basalt is so hard, erosion can hardly make a mark on it. Perhaps the only thing left to do to change the endless basalt is to cover it up. Glaciers, gigantic floods, and windblown dust did that. To complete this picture, throw in some volcanoes. Voila! Washington State.

Just 60 miles north of Cashmere, near Methow, the peaks soften and begin rolling out to the eastern plains.

CHAPTER
2

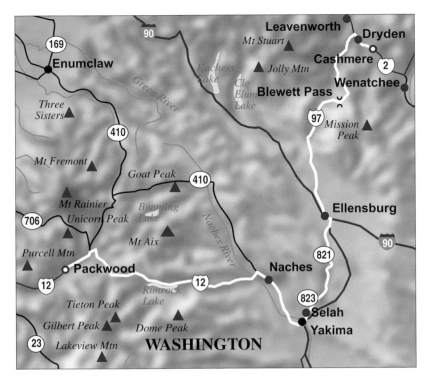

Into this geological wonderland a bike comes wandering. Your bike. You can see all these wonders in this next journey from **Packwood** to **Cashmere.**

From Packwood you will journey east on U.S. 12. You will roll down the shoulders of **Mt. Rainier** over its much drier east side. The forests dramatically change from ferns and Douglas firs to pines and alpine firs. Descending from **White Pine Pass,** a winter ski area, you can see smaller volcanoes and folded mountains far below.

The first time I rode this highway, I was perched on an unfamiliar rented bike. The highway has only a thin guardrail between the road and deep canyon below. I nervously carved each turn, trying to watch the scenery and still maintain a safe speed. Somehow I noticed I was going faster and faster and seeing less and less. Knowing I was exceeding the highest possible speed with which this road could be navigated, I was surprised when a chopper with ape hangers passed me on a blind turn. I kept waiting to see the remains of his bike attached to the front of an oncoming SUV or a smear of orange paint on guardrail somewhere. I'm guessing the fellow made it safely down to **Yakima.** But I decided to slow down and enjoy the forest and mountains more.

CHAPTER

2

The Route From Packwood

0   Start in Packwood going east on U.S. Highway 12

72   Merge onto Interstate 82 north toward Ellensburg/Selah. Get into the left lane.

73.7 Take exit 30a onto Washington Highway 823 north toward Selah. This is a left exit ramp.

77.2 Stay on 823 north. Merge onto 821 North.

101.7 Turn right on Thrall Road toward the freeway

102.3 Take the U.S. 97 north/ Interstate 82 north ramp

110.2 Take the U.S. 97 north exit (exit number 106)

162.4 Turn right onto U.S. 2 toward Cashmere

168.7 Arrive in Cashmere

Soon you will find yourself on the edge of **Rimrock Lake,** a six-mile-long reservoir formed in 1925 when the **Tieton Dam** was built. At one end a tiny store, with a well-used bathroom around back, made me wonder if it was built the same year as the dam.

Quickly after leaving Rimrock Lake, you will notice the trees almost disappear and desert shrubs pop up. Mt. Rainier keeps most of the Pacific moisture on its west side. The dusty town of **Naches** has services like gas, food, and lodging. If you want anything other than the simplest food and lodging in this area, turn left (west) onto WA 410. About 20 miles up the road is **Whistlin' Jack Lodge** with a chef, cabins, and motel rooms.

Pulling out of Naches, go east on U.S. 12. You may find this road busy with big trucks and increasingly suburban traffic as you approach Yakima. About 12 miles outside of Naches, keep an eye out for I-82, toward Selah/ Ellensburg. Stay on I-82 for about two miles and take the 823 N exit (exit 30a) toward **Selah.** Stay on 823 as it merges into 821 North toward **Ellensburg.** You are in for a treat.

Most of the automobile traffic is running parallel to you on I-82, while you are sweeping through the **Yakima River Valley** on a graceful riverside road. The golden grass covered hills to the west look fuzzy and soft. They are huge heaps of glacial gravel left by the ice age floods. I never get tired of seeing the cold blue river, golden hills, and soft blue sky. The state police drive tan, dust-colored patrol cars with friendly, helpful troopers who do not tolerate speeding. Watch for rocks on the road near cliffs.

CHAPTER

2

Amazingly hard basalt cliffs give evidence that simple water can cut through thousands of years of volcanic flows.

Leavenworth was but a simple logging town; now it has embraced a Bavarian theme that draws visitors from all over the world.

**CHAPTER
2**

Not far from Cashmere, a Columbia River vineyard soaks up the sun and nutrients from the volcanic/river silt soil mix. Washington State wines sell well.

Ellensburg was built in the **Kittitas Valley** and prides itself for its location, central to touring the many Yakima Valley wineries. Remember that basalt flow I told you about covering most of the state of Washington? Basalt covers ancient and glacial gravel. The Kittitas Valley allows the winds to blow through fiercely at times. It was here I learned that a Harley Road King is superior to a Honda Goldwing in serious crosswinds.

As you approach Ellensburg from the south on 821, keep in mind your goal is 97 north toward **Wenatchee.** Stay on 821 north until you get to Thrall Road. Turn right here, go about a half mile and merge onto 97 north (also called I-82 north). After eight miles on this highway, you will take the 97 north exit toward Wenatchee.

Once you are on 97 north, the winds seem to quickly fade as you pass by pretty farms and rural scenes. You are on your way to **Blewett Pass.** U.S. 97 in this area has broad sweeping turns, pretty views of forests and mountains. It's all quick four-lane driving unless you get behind a clump of RVs or heavy trucks.

Blewett Pass is famous for 55-million-year-old fossilized palms and flowers, thousand dollar gold nuggets (in earlier times), and beautiful mountain views. It's about 60 miles from Ellensburg to the junction of 2. Turn east (right) on 2 and take the second Cashmere exit (Cotlets Way) to find the motel. I always stay in Cashmere because nearby **Leavenworth** has so many tourists that the room prices are often higher.

Cashmere used to be called Mission, but changed its name in 1904 to its present name after the beautiful Vale of Kashmir in India. The best food in this part of Washington is the **Walnut Café** (reservations recommended—even for lunch) about two blocks from the motel. It's a bit on the gourmet side. If you want simple, downhome food and don't mind a little smoke in your eye, **Barney's Tavern** has great breakfasts and big, simple dinners. Another place with good home cooking is the **Big Y.** Get back on 2 north toward Leavenworth. You'll see the Big Y about five miles up the road on the right just past **Dryden.**

The green willows offer a break to rock, sky, and river in this Yakima River view.

CHAPTER
2

Located on a major fault (called the **Leavenworth Fault**) and surrounded by sharp mountains, the nearby town of Leavenworth is a marvel of geological and economic wonders. Several years ago Leavenworth decided to go with a Bavarian theme rather than turn into a ghost town when the timber industry started to fade. The results are startling. What started as a few Bavarian-style false fronted stores is now a booming Bavarian business center. You may not find pot holders and ceramic plates celebrating Noah and the flood, but there are lots of items with the image of King Ludwig II.

Cashmere Food and Lodging

Walnut Café
(509) 782-2022

Barney's Tavern
(509) 782-3637

Big Y Café
(509) 5487580

Perhaps these hills don't look like much, but just beyond them lie the nearly impenetrable Northern Cascade Mountains.

CHAPTER
2

Bikers meet at dawn in the Columbia Gorge for an unforgettable ride.

Village Inn Motel
(509) 782-3522
(800) 793-3522

Whistlin' Jack Lodge
(800) 827 2299
www.whistlinjacks.com

CHAPTER
2

B.C.: Where the Natives Bike

Remember that feeling you got when your mom dropped you off someplace, like a new school, for the first time? She drove off and you momentarily wondered if you should run after her calling to come back. Far from home and on your own, it exhilarated and left you thinking about where you really belonged. When you enter Canada for the first time, you may feel like that. The signs, gas stations, money—all are different.

As soon as the road rolls out ahead of you, the differences become part of the magic. As a motorcyclist, you'll know this is the place you should be riding.

View of Highway 12 from Lytton to Lillooet. I love this highway.

Sunset view of islands near Tofino. Listen carefully for the bird calls and faraway chug of a fishing boat.

When you think of British Columbia, don't images of vast pristine forests come to mind? How about great arid deserts where camels were once used to haul gold miners from water hole to water hole? This didn't sound right to me either, until I saw it for myself. Beautiful dry rock lands ribboned with biker-friendly highways and tourist-ready towns lay hidden in British Columbia.

You can tell by the way I've neglected describing urban centers in this book that I'm not really a city boy. Give me the two-lane road and the country café. Despite this, I love **Vancouver B.C.**—a city surrounded on three sides by water and four sides by 180 parks, gardens, museums, shopping, and the most urbane acceptance of individuality this side of San Francisco. You can be a biker or whatever you want, folks just accept you for who you are. I love this town!

From Vancouver you can rent a bike and go from Canada's San Francisco-style sophistication to a wild west/gold rush desert town of **Cache Creek.** Along the way there's **Hell's Gate Airtram** over a startlingly narrow gorge through which 200 million gallons of water surges, the movie-set-like town of **Hope,** the drama of the magnificent **Fraser River Canyon,** and the rustic, remote roads and towns of this part of British Columbia.

On the west side of British Columbia, there's the surprise town of **Tofino** teetering on the edge of the great North American continent balanced on the edge of Vancouver Island. Perhaps some of the best food anywhere in the whole Pacific Northwest is found in Tofino. If you take a kayak tour, you can eagle-watch among the secret water pathways among the many islands surrounding Tofino. To get there you need to travel an unforgettable road that will haunt you long after you are safe at home. There's no doubt that the best way to travel the B. C. Ferries is by motorcycle.

Slipping up the **Sea-to-Sky Highway** past the green waters of **Howe Sound,** you'll see a gigantic rock, **The Chief,** that draws rock climbers like a Harley parked inside a shopping mall draws gawkers. Just when you think you are in the true wilderness, you come upon **Whistler:** a Disneyland for travelers who love shopping designer boutique-style-stores and people watching. Between Whistler and **Lillooet** you ride some of the most scenic roads anyone has ever ridden in North America. Rustic innocence, glowing blue glaciers, pencil thin white waterfalls across the canyons, lusty wild flowers blooming with abandon for all to see, terrific pavement and light traffic, I want to ride this road right now.

For Americans, Canada represents an ideal clean innocence to which we'd like to return. Once you spend a little time in British Columbia, the home-like feel will grow and become part of you. Long after your trip you'll think about a place to go that's pleasant, home-like and exhilarating: British Columbia.

Maturing eagle chicks watch life from the boughs of ancient trees near Tofino.

CHAPTER
3

Trip 6 Portland to Nelson to Condon

A Columbia River Basin Journey to Canada

Distance *913 miles without side trips (four days, three nights; longer if hot, windy, or rainy)*

Terrain *Mostly rural highways, some straight, boring interstates, most of the turns are gentle and sweeping. Twisties near Condon have few blind turns. Watch for deer, rocks near cliffs, farm traffic, and heat.*

Highlights *Columbia River Gorge, Horse Heaven Hills, Grand Coulee Dam, Dry Falls, Canada, Lake Roosevelt, Harrington-Tokio Road, and roads near Condon.*

Banks Lake was created to keep the turbines of Grand Coulee Dam turning during hours of peak demand. Can you picture the Great Missoula Flood roaring down this canyon?

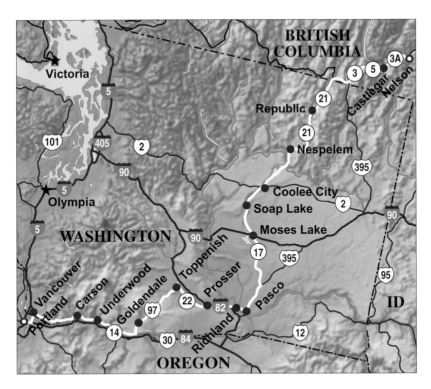

The deepest lake in America is **Crater Lake** at 1932 feet. It's six miles across. Is that a lot of water? Not compared to **Lake Missoula.** Think about a lake 2,000 feet deep and over 200 miles across. That's a lot of water!

Lake Missoula had a little problem. Ice floats. Since the dam holding all that water back was made of glacial ice. . . one day it floated. Now imagine a gigantic flood traveling at over 90 mph, its waters laden with silt and Goldwing-sized rocks. In two days it carried 10 times the modern output for all the rivers on earth. This catastrophic flood happened dozens of times.

This flood left the land perfect for motorcycle touring. Not only for the scenic aspects of the ravaged countryside, but the beauty of the hills, valleys and coulees. To really appreciate the effects of the Lake Missoula floods and to have a terrific motorcycle trip, I'm going to take you along the **Columbia River** into **Nelson, Canada.**

Begin this journey near **Portland** by crossing over to the Washington side of the Columbia. Take Highway 14 up the stunning natural beauty of the **Columbia River Gorge.** Many locals claim that Highway 14 is one of the best motorcycle roads in the Pacific Northwest for its scenery, its sweeping curves, and the rapid climate changes along its route.

CHAPTER

3

The Route From Portland to Nelson

0   Portland to Interstate 84 east toward The Dalles

5   Turn north onto Interstate 205 toward Vancouver

11   Turn east onto Highway 14 toward Camas

103   Turn north onto Highway 97 toward Goldendale

162   Turn right (east) onto Highway 223/23 toward Prosser

193   Merge onto Highway 12. You will be on several freeways, but just keep following the signs toward Pasco/Spokane

227   You should be on 395. Follow signs to Moses Lake/Highway 17

250   Turn onto Highway 17 toward Moses Lake

336   Take 155 toward Electric City/Grand Coulee

362   At Nespelem look for the signs toward Republic

378   Turn left (north) onto Highway 21

446   At the Canadian border, follow signs to Grand Forks

477   Stay on Provincial Highway 3 toward Castlegar. Merge onto Highway 3A toward Nelson

509   Arrive at Nelson

The Route From Nelson to Condon

0   From Nelson, go south on 6 toward Salmo

23   Go west onto Highway 3 toward Castlegar. Follow the signs to Trail/Rossland. You will exit Highway 3

31   From Trail, follow the signs to Rossland/Paterson. Highway 22

43   Follow Highway 25 along Lake Roosevelt

169   At Harrington, take the Harrington-Tokio Road south toward Ritzville

186   At Ritzville, take 395 south toward Kennewick

203   Take the exit toward Pasco/Wallula (Highway 12 east). Follow signs toward Hermiston. This will take you on 730 and 207

298   From Hermiston stay on 207 to Heppner

341   From Heppner, follow 207 to 206 to Condon

The farther east you go, the drier the climate becomes. By the time you reach **Goldendale,** the summertime colors are mostly golds and temperatures climb.

You might want to stop at the quirky **Maryhill Museum.** Besides the art and historical exhibits, the museum buildings are striking both in design and location. A full sized replica of Stonehenge stands just east of the main museum. Wealthy businessman Sam Hill built this huge stone structure in 1918 to honor World War I soldiers.

This area can be quite hot for a biker, so care should be exercised as you travel.

From Goldendale, I suggest you take Highway 97 north to **Toppenish.** This veers away from the Columbia River, but you must see the **Horse Heaven Hills.** This crescent-shaped region covers more than 600,000 acres along its 60-mile length. Travelers might think that these are piles of gravel deposited by the Missoula Floods. Geologists think these are folded hills. They seem so soft and strong from the saddle of a bike. I never tire of looking at them.

These travelers wait their turn to talk with Canadian Customs at Carson, B.C. Just beyond this crossing, there's soft grass for napping and clean bathrooms.

CHAPTER

3

10 Rules for Hot Weather and Desert Riding

1. Hydrate yourself. Experts say you should begin drinking water the night before the ride. This allows you to store up liquid. Alcohol and caffeine act as diuretics. One cup of coffee or an alcoholic drink is like pulling the plug on the bathtub. Your body will drain all your stored liquid leaving you vulnerable to the heat. If you need the caffeine to stay alert, you should not be on the road.

2. Wear your armored jacket and pants. Picture the outside temperature as something that you want to keep away from your skin. To do this, you wear your jacket and pants and use evaporative cooling to control your body temperature. This may seem counter-intuitive, but if you cover your body, wrapping the exposed parts in wet cloth, the resulting evaporation can actually make you chilled as you ride across super-heated pavement. I wear a wet neck cloth and a wet sweatshirt under my vented jacket and a Cool Mate Pump (www.aerostich.com) to keep my sweatshirt wet.

3. Leave at dawn. Take advantage of the cooler air and lighter traffic. If you start at dawn, your body will not even miss your caffeine. Watch out for animals, which may be more active during this time. By 1:00 p.m. you have your whole day's riding already done and the pick of the motels. Take a shower and a nap while other bikers fight the heat.

4. Monitor tire air pressure. When tires have low pressure, they quickly heat up. Check tire pressure and bike fluids regularly to avoid a catastrophic equipment failure. Test any bike modifications prior to heading out to the desert.

5. Wear good boots. The air near the pavement can be so hot, it can actually cook your feet.

6. Wear a full face helmet, and keep the visor closed. Since you have a quarter of your blood supply in your head at any given moment, keep it protected from the heat. To test this suggestion, on a hot day put on your helmet with the visor open and blast your face with a hot hair dryer. Then close the visor and blast your face. Which is better? If your face is sweaty, open the vent until it's dry.

7. Listen to your body. Headache, nausea, and muscle cramps are the harbingers of heat exhaustion. If untreated, this can be fatal. Take a break, cool off, and drink lots of water if any of these physical symptoms occur.

8. Drink water frequently. Your body needs a pint per hour and regular light meals. Sweating people need the food to replace electrolytes they lose. Sports drinks are OK, but water and food are best. Pop has large amounts of sugar and chemicals that do not help keep your body cool. It is a poor substitute for water. Avoid junk food.

9. Be prepared. Check the list of safety gear. If riding with friends, much of this can be spread amongst all the riders.

10. Watch your speed. You might think that the desert is the best place to really find the top speed of your bike. Never outrun your ability to stop to avoid a road hazard. Desert cliffs and bushes regularly deposit rocks, animals, and RVs in the fast lane. Also, besides being expensive, who wants to stand out in the blazing heat listening to a patrol person explain the hazards of excessive speed. Ride safely.

Hot Weather Trip Gear:

armored, vented jacket
armored pants
sturdy boots
gloves
full-face helmet
first aid kit
umbrella or space blanket for emergency shade
cell phone or FRS/CB radio
water (lots)
neck cloth
sun block lip protector
sunscreen
sun hat to wear during breaks
reflective vest for riding in the dark or during early morning hours
tool kit
tire repair kit
flashlight
air pump
maps
tire gauge
one-a-day type vitamins with minerals

The road from Goldendale to Toppenish is a 60 mile stretch without services. Make sure you have plenty of gas before starting out. You will pass through the **Yakima Indian Reservation** and a sparse pine forest before blasting out to where you can see the Horse Heaven Hills.

Turn east on Highway 22 to parallel the Yakima River. You can spend the night in Prosser or any of the rural towns in this area. The motels tend to be clean and cheap. Ask around for a good restaurant. Typically each town has a Mexican, Chinese, and café restaurant. Many have taverns, which can sometimes offer good road food.

To continue this journey, you will need to traverse a congested area where the **Yakima** and **Snake Rivers** enter the Columbia. This is the **Richland/Kennewick/Pasco** region, often called Tri-cities. Your goal is to get through this crowed area and up to Highway 395 going north. To do this, I just keep following the signs to Spokane until I'm out of town.

View of Columbia River Gorge from Cape Horn.
This place is so photogenic, it will suck the memory
from your digital camera.

Once the greatest waterfall in the world, now this area is called Dry Falls. The silence is so vast, you can imagine the roar. Look for this on your right after you pass Soap Lake.

Once on 395 heading north, you might notice that the road is somewhat boring, hot, and straight. You will merge onto Highway 17 toward **Moses Lake.** Perhaps the floods flattened this area, but I find it a bit entertaining to dodge onions and potatoes dropped on the roads by the ubiquitous produce trucks.

A stop at **Bob's Café,** just off the freeway in Moses Lake, is always worthwhile. They'll give you an omelet the size of a football and pancakes the size of a Vespa wheel. Moses Lake, dug out of the valley by the floods, is the marker that the roads are about to become the stuff of legends. About 20 miles away is **Soap Lake,** the start of at least two days of terrific roads and gorgeous sights. Get your camera ready.

Be sure to stop at **Dry Falls**—what's left of the world's largest waterfalls. Nearby, the mysteries of ancient magma, floods, and sediment have left

Steamboat Rock seems to float in Banks Lake. With day use and over 150 campsites, this state park is perfect for sun worshippers.

other sights. Eons ago hot magma filled spaces underground and set slowly into hard, mammoth rocks. When the surrounding sediment wore away, steep sided, flat-topped mesas were left. One startling example of such a basalt butte is **Steamboat Rock.** With a surface area of more than 600 acres and a height of 800 feet, it dominates the landscape.

I suggest you spend the night in **Grand Coulee City.** The friendly people at the **Trail West Motel** will offer you old towels to clean up your dusty bike.

In this glorious part of Washington, engineers designed a dam about a mile long and as tall as a 42-story building. At 9:30 nightly during August the spillways open up, sending a gigantic wall of white roaring water over the top. This white wall forms the "screen" for a 40-minute laser light show with patriotic themes and music featuring the story of **Grand Coulee Dam.** Want to see a 3,000-foot-long eagle? Here's the place.

Follow State Highway 155 out of Grand Coulee City like you are going north to **Omak,** but as soon as you get to **Nespelem,** look for the hidden sign for the road to **Republic.** This road, called the Cache Creek Road, may appear as a dirt road on your map, but locals know it as a fine, paved biking road: heavily wooded with graceful, banked turns.

When you arrive at State Highway 21, turn north toward Republic. This beautiful, forested road follows the **Sandpoil River** past farms and grazing land. The high, rocky cliffs seem to close in on you as you motor up the road. I really wondered how the road would get through. A tunnel? Suddenly you are through the canyons in a narrow spot where the river cut through. The land flattens out and you roll into Republic—a biker friendly town where you can get a great breakfast at **The Sportsmen Roost.**

Ripe wheat turns the world to yellow along the Tokio Road between Harrington and Ritzville.

Canada Travel

Customs

Those of us who've lived near Canada for years know all you need is a driver's license to ride back and forth across the border. Since 9/11, some things have changed. Border guards are under orders to be more careful. Now we always travel with our passports. If you don't have a passport, your birth certificate works well.

Picture this scene: you and your bride have just finished a tour of Tofino and are heading back to the U.S.A. You need to be back at work on Monday. Someone in Washington announces we've gone Code Orange and the borders suddenly get very tight. You could be stuck in Canada.

Canadian customs may turn away visitors who have committed such crimes as DUI or domestic abuse. Call Canadian Customs at (204) 983-3500 or (506) 636-5064 during office hours to inquire about any concerns you may have about this.

Canadians do not like visitors to bring in weapons: guns, stun guns, mace, pepper spray. They don't care about knives unless you are in an airport. Customs agents will also ask you about alcohol or gifts you are bringing. They want to know where you are going and how long you plan to be there.

If you get into an accident, they want to see your insurance cards. You can request an international card from your insurance company. Usually these are free.

Speed and Distances

Years ago Canada switched to the metric system, leaving the United States as practically the only place in the world which still uses standard measurements. Short of a math class, there are some simple ways to approximate amounts.

A mile is .6 kilometers. That means when you see a speed limit like 30 kph, to find the standard equivalent, multiply by six. Thirty times six is 180. Drop the zero to get 18 mph. If you are on the road to Tofino, obey the speed limit suggestions.

Don't know your six times tables? You can also look at your bike's speedometer. It has mph and kph. If the sign says a place is 100 km away, look at your speedometer, find 100 kph and see what the mph mark is at this same spot: 60. Therefore 100 kilometers is 60 miles.

Weight

Want to buy some cheese for your loaf of bread? How much to order at the deli? Canadians use kilograms and grams. 1,000gm = 1kg. So what do you do if you want 1/4 pound of that sharp cheddar? Since a kilogram is a bit more than two pounds, 500g is little more than a pound. You want 125g to get about a 1/4 pound. If this seems confusing, just tell the deli clerk it's for a sandwich.

Money

Use your credit card to pay for gas, food, and lodging. Each time you change money from one country to another, you pay an exchange fee. The lowest fees possible are though your credit card. I always pick up $100 in Canadian cash at a bank ATM. Make sure you take your ATM card to a bank, not a quickie money exchange place, but an honest to goodness bank with a regular ATM machine. I use my credit card as much as possible until the end of the journey, when I try to use up all my Canadian money.

Nelson, B.C. is a great place to people watch and shop for something Canadian to bring home.

CHAPTER
3

Canada 1, a highway to heavenly views of knife edged mountains, deep forests, and steep V canyons.

CHAPTER
3

Once you cross the border, Canada Highway 3 starts off rough and poorly paved, but will soon change into one of the nicest touring highways of the trip. Well engineered and packed with beautiful views of vast forests and knife edged mountains, it takes you to another world.

You might run into bikers staying in the **Heritage Inn** at Nelson. They serve the best breakfast in town, and Nelson has shopping so you can pick up souvenirs for friends unlucky enough that they couldn't come along.

Nelson is the apex of this journey. I suggest you head back on Canadian Highway 6, then turn off toward the industrial town of **Trail** in order to see the Old West face of **Rossland** and to reconnect with the Columbia River. From there you enter the United States at **Paterson.**

From here you motor along **Lake Roosevelt** for 90 miles and then pass through several rural Washington towns on your way to **Ritzville.** The most prosperous town is **Davenport**—clean and justifiably proud of its schools. Other towns may have boarded up bowling alleys and other sad buildings.

When you think of a great bike road, what comes to mind? Twisties? Gentle, well-banked highways? Great views? On the map, the Harrington Tokio Road looks like none of these. Yet it should turn out to be a high point of your trip. The road rolls through bright yellow wheat fields covering steep, cultivated hills. Climbing up and down the hills, a biker often finds himself alone with just three colors: vivid yellow wheat, pure blue sky, and fresh black pavement. It's an odd and exciting feeling to have such intense colors in such abundance. I think only a biker would notice this.

If you spend the night in Ritzville, I have two pieces of advice: stay in the **Best Western Bronco Inn Motel** and don't eat anywhere but the **Circle T Restaurant.** The motel is brand new and comfortable. It has in-room air conditioners so you can have it make noise all night if you are sleeping with a snoring buddy. You can peek out the window anytime to check your bike.

The Columbia River Basin drains an area about the size of France, or about 258,000 square miles. On this journey you can discover desert, mountain, forest, rural and urban roads. You can scrape your floor boards on twisties and lean through beautiful banked sweepers. You can pass through ancient volcanic burial grounds and young, upstart folded mountains. But the most exciting motorcycle roads are just ahead of you.

From Ritzville, head south toward Kennewick/Pasco. Once near **Pasco,** watch for the signs for Highway 12 toward **Wallula** and **Hermiston.** Here you travel around an elbow of the Columbia River. What beautiful country! The stacked up basalt slabs making up the cliffs along either side of the great river reveal thousands of years of basalt flows.

CHAPTER

3

Your map may show Tokio Road, running between Harrington and Ritzville, as perfectly straight, but as you can see here, it climbs up and down perfect, rounded hills.

From Hermiston, make your way to **Heppner.** Stop here for a break and to catch your breath. Heppner is the gateway to biking nirvana. During your break, you can call ahead to the **Condon Motel** to book your room. The 29 miles between Heppner and **Condon** is a two-lane rural highway winding gently through golden hills and rocky bluffs. The pavement seems new and the curves helpfully reveal their apexes and links so a biker could easily get into that zone that only bikers know. This is my favorite road in all the Pacific Northwest.

In Condon you can walk the four blocks to the **Country Café** from your motel room. Few people have ever finished eating one of their famous chicken fried steaks.

This journey only lasts two days, the time it takes to drain 500 cubic miles of water from **Lake Missoula** through the Columbia River Basin, a basin now filled with dry waterfalls, golden folded hills, a massive dam, a 90-mile-long lake, interesting rural towns, and terrific motorcycle roads. If a rider had some time after landing in Condon, that person could link up with the journey to Ontario (Trip 21) and the wonders of the John Day area.

Grand Coulee Dam Light Show

For show times and details:
www.grandcouleedam.org/

Food and Lodging

Trail West Motel
(866) 633-8157
www.trailwestmotel.com/

Bob's Café
Moses Lake, WA
(509) 765-3211

Sportsmen Roost
Republic, WA
(509) 775-0404

Best Western Bronco Inn
Ritzville, WA
(509) 659-5000

Trip 7 British Columbia Joy Ride

From Vancouver To Hope to Cache Creek

Distance *210 miles*

Terrain *Gentle sweeping turns along the Fraser River, mostly four lanes of traffic. Canada Highway 1 is the artery between Vancouver and all points east. Summer attracts tourists to this beautiful highway. Even so, you will have the whole road to yourself at some points. Some rocks near cliff faces, watch for deer and other forest animals, especially near dawn and dusk*

Highlights *Scenic views of mountains, farms, canyons, and towns along the Fraser River. A look at the only desert in all of British Columbia*

After leaving Lytton, this traveler tries to stop grinning as he heads through the dry mountains toward Lillooet.

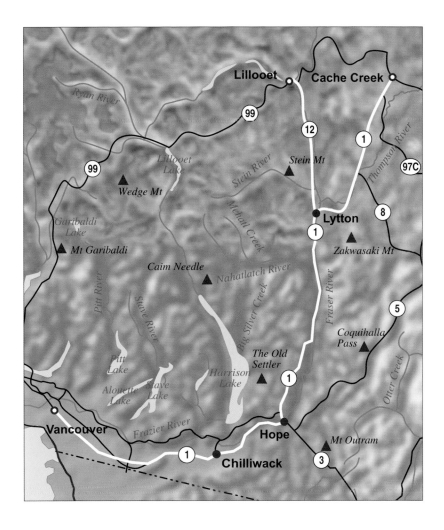

The Route From Vancouver to Lillooet via Hope

0 Leave Vancouver on Highway 1 going east

161 Turn left onto Highway 12

200 Arrive in Lillooet

The Route From Vancouver to Cache Creek via Hope

0 Leave Vancouver on Highway 1 going east

209 Arrive in Cache Creek

CHAPTER

3

The shining city of Vancouver, surrounded by water, gracefully and warmly welcomes everyone.

Have you ever been to an amazing place? The views, the atmosphere, the sounds, tastes, and smells keep your adrenaline pumping full blast and your brain is awash with endorphins. Such euphoria! And the locals don't even look up. It's all so much pretty wallpaper to them. Holy cow! I want to shake them and scream, "Notice this!" When you take this journey, you'll notice this wallpaper phenomena over this whole striking ride. But you have the advantage of being a visitor who takes joy in these special places.

You will pull out of the sparkling city of **Vancouver,** the taste of perfect coffee on your lips. After a brief but annoyingly familiar fight through suburban traffic as you travel east on Highway 1, you will find yourself on a freeway blasting through the **Fraser River Valley.** Looking at a map, you might wonder why I don't send you on Highway 7, which runs parallel to Hwy. 1. If you enjoy multiple stoplights and a flood of suburban strip-mall, hurry-up traffic, be my guest. Highway 7 does get pretty nice after it finally frees itself from the suburbs, but I like getting to the good part quickly.

CHAPTER

3

The good part. This is what the locals don't seem to notice. Just 50 miles from the city, you will see the pretty farms with salt and pepper shaker mountains plopped down randomly. The farms are well tended, the cattle passively graze, and the crops grow with lust in their twiney hearts—unashamedly enjoying the long Canadian summer days. Always in the background, sharp-edged mountains creep closer as the miles click by. It's when I pass **Chilliwack** that I finally feel I'm out in the boonies. It seems people in cars don't see any of this.

You'll observe the great **Fraser River** on your left. Look at it closely; it will become an important part of your ride over the next day or so. Named after Simon Fraser, the Canadian explorer version of Lewis and Clark, this mighty river flows nearly 800 miles through steep, narrow canyons and broad valleys. Lucky for bikers, Highway 1 follows it closely mile upon mile.

After Fraser explored this region, the gold seekers and railroad company opened it up for everyone else. One of the towns supplying both groups was **Hope.**

The Fraser River cuts though hard rock mountains. The construction of the railroad line proved to be an amazing feat of engineering.

CHAPTER

3

Once you pull into Hope the tug of the mountains on your handlebars will urge you to hurry on, but Hope makes a good rest stop. There are plenty of modest motels and you can get a great meal at **Darrell's Place.** If the town looks familiar to movie buffs, *Rambo: First Blood* was filmed in town, as well as other pictures.

Once you are out of Hope, the roads remain four-lanes in most areas, but occasionally it will narrow to two. The **Fraser River,** a silty-milky-dusty-brown, flows below. One roadside attraction you will see is the **Hell's Gate** tourist area. For a fee, you can take a tram down over the narrowest part of the Fraser River to a restaurant/observation deck.

Here you can lick an ice cream cone and learn about how the gold rush and the construction of the train line changed the area. You can look at the dramatic torrent of water—a flow twice that of Niagara Falls—and wonder how a blind cow ever made it through alive. This is one place where you do not need to urge people to notice their environment; this canyon demands a visitor's attention.

When you get to **Lytton,** a pretty town with blah food and interesting views, you can see where the Fraser River and the **Thompson River** join. You can tool around and look at the clean houses, the proud caboose in the town park, and the historical sites. Then you need to make a decision. You can either continue on Highway 1 to **Cache Creek** or take the twisty Highway 12 to **Lillooet.**

The Hell's Gate roadside attraction captures visitors as they innocently travel the Canada 1 Highway north toward Cache Creek.

CHAPTER

3

*Sometimes views of the Fraser River Canyon will make you wish you could fly.
Luckily for bikers, we nearly always feel like we are flying.*

There are several advantages to taking Highway 1 out of Lytton. You follow the Thompson River on sweeping turns through a naked desert. Viewing
the bare hills, you understand why camels were imported to help bring out
the gold during the end of the 19th century. The sharp British Columbia
rocks were too much for the tender feet of camels, so the experiment was
dropped.

Once you get to the Cache Creek turnoff, you'll see the **Hat Creek
Ranch** (good food), said to be the most haunted place in B.C. Cache Creek
also has plenty of services for the traveler. Supposedly, it also has a creekside cache of stolen gold buried by an 1880s robber. No one knows exactly
where the gold was buried, but a visitor has as much chance to find it as anyone.

A nice place to eat in Cache Creek is the **Bearclaw Lodge.** Also, the
Sandman Motel serves breakfast all day in a Denny's-style restaurant. For a
town with a population of only about 1,000, Cache Creek has plenty of lodging.

CHAPTER
3

This shot was taken a bit north of Boston Bar.

Another advantage of staying on Highway 1 is that you can follow it all the way to **Banff.** The eight-hour (non-stop) journey from Cache Creek to Banff runs by the **Canadian Rockies** and heart-stopping views of jagged peaks hanging within a sea of crystal atmosphere. It will not seem like a real place to you. Motels fill quickly along this busy summer route. Get reservations or be off the highway by three.

Let's say you decide not to make the run to Cache Creek. My favorite road in Lytton is Highway 12, to Lillooet: a sparsely traveled two-lane road winding through canyons and desert. This is the kind of highway I like to ride. On Highway 12 from Lytton, the transition from forested mountain to arid, hilly desert completes itself. Most visitors riding this lonely, winding way deep in British Columbia find it odd to see high brown desert mountains. Isn't B.C. all about forests?

When you arrive at Cache Creek or Lillooet, you can link up with the **Sea to Sky Highway** through **Whistler** (Trip 9). Whichever route you choose, I'm sure you will notice the startling beauty around you. If it starts to become wallpaper, take a break, a deep breath, and drink in British Columbia's treasures: mountains, forest, canyons, clean air, history, and the feeling of being in British Columbia.

The clear white thread of a distant waterfall pulls the camera lens toward it.
The air in this place feels soft and clean.

CHAPTER
3

The browny-greens of the river will turn silver at sunset. Stick around.

Cache Creek Food and Lodging

Bear Claw Lodge
(250) 457-9705
(888) 552-2528
(Breakfast, lunch, and dinner)

Nugget Road Motel
(250) 457-9300
(Budget lodging)

CHAPTER
3

Good Knight Inn
(800) 736-5588
www.goodknightinn.com
(Nice lodging)

Hat Creek Ranch
(800) 782-0922
www.hatcreekranch.com
(Food and lodging)

Sandman Inn
(250) 457-6284
(Denny's style food)

Bill Ma's Restaurant
(250) 457-9268

Husky House Restaurant
(250) 457-9312|

North End Restaurant
(250) 457-6261

Hope

Darrell's Place
(604) 869-3708

Home Restaurant
(604) 869-5558

Red Roof Inn
(604) 869-2446
(800) 667-4070 (in British Columbia and Alberta)

Lake of the Woods Resort Motel
(604) 869-9211

Skagit Motel
(604) 869-5220

CHAPTER
3

Trip 8 British Columbia Island Vacation

Vancouver to Tofino

Distance *170 miles, 35 on the ferry (6.5 hours total)*

Terrain *Pleasant winding roads through forests and beside lakes and streams. Some annoying suburban traffic near Nanaimo. The 50 miles just prior to Tofino are some of the worst paved roads I've ever ridden. Hazards include deer, rocks, and curb-sized sunken grades. If taken slow, no more dangerous than any mountain road.*

Highlights *Tofino! International village in a far and remote place. End of the earth feel. Salty vistas of tree topped islands, eagles and other birds. Terrific food.*

The west coast of Vancouver Island is so rocky, the few beaches that do exist are considered treasures.

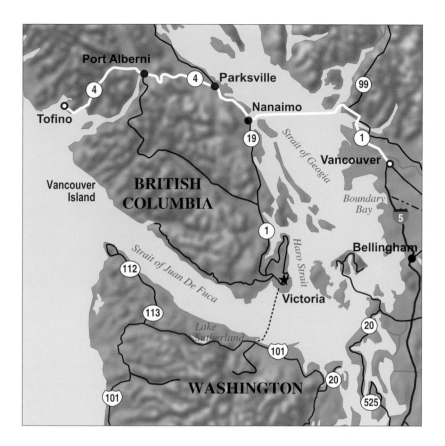

The Route From Vancouver

0   Begin at Vancouver and go west on Canada Highway 1. Follow signs for Horseshoe Bay ferry docks. As you approach the "end" of Canada Highway 1, the name of the road is changed to Provincial Highway 99. Continue west on 99.

10   Board the Nanaimo Ferry. This ride usually lasts 95 minutes after leaving the dock. When you leave the ferry, follow the signs to Highway 19 going north.

35   Go northwest on Highway 4 toward Port Alberni.

135   Arrive in Tofino

Bikers await the signal to board the ferry. Most of these bikers are locals who commute with their bikes.

Imagine you are biking through intense forests and remote lakes on your way to a small town perched upon a rocky peninsula. The condition of the road tells you it's not often traveled. What would you expect to find at the end of this long forest path through trackless woods and pristine lakes? There were no roads to this area before the 1950s, and I expected a picturesque fishing or logging village clinging to the rocky shore. On my first visit, I became more confident in these expectations as I approached the town.

When you first view **Tofino,** the panorama of glassy seas, dozens of tree-capped rocky islands, and wheeling birds will far exceed your expectations. Tofino, named for a Spanish admiral and situated at the end of a long road, calls to visitors.

Visitors answer the call and flock to this forested, rocky peninsula. There sits the pretty town, looking prosperous like an older grand dame proudly wearing her prettiest clothes. What you might not expect are the tourists: dozens of outdoor cafés and restaurants are jammed with travelers enjoying the mild summer day, blue sky, and ambiance of a relaxing getaway. Where do they all come from? The narrow road here could not possibly support all these travelers. Could the masses come from the constant flow of small sea planes? No. I still don't know how they all get there.

These travelers may have picked Tofino by looking at a map of **Vancouver Island.** This island is huge—about half the size of Mexico. Despite this size, there are relatively few paved roads. Almost none of the roads on the Pacific Ocean side of the island are paved. So perhaps these visitors looked at the map and noticed that of the three or four Pacific towns accessible by paved road, the most remote appears to be Tofino.

Coming from the city of Vancouver, a traveler must go west on Canada's Highway 1 to Horseshoe Bay. Following the ferry signs, that person would get into the ferry line to **Nanaimo.** Since bikes are loaded onto ferries first, after paying the fare, the biker would be directed ahead of all the car traffic to the front of the ferry lines.

After a 95-minute ferry ride, exit the ferry onto Highway 19 going north toward **Parksville.** For me, this is the least enjoyable part of the trip. Wouldn't you expect to be on lazy island roads at this point? No such luck. You are on busy suburban stop-light, strip-mall, fast-food-joint, hurry-up roads until Hwy 19 becomes a freeway about 10 miles from the ferry dock. Even on the freeway, life is too busy until you finally take the Highway 4 exit toward **Port Alberni.**

View from the Wild Pacific Trail out of Ucluelet. You need to get off the bike to see this.

CHAPTER

3

As the kilometers roll by, the road becomes increasingly enjoyable and island-like. You'll pass through the **Tsahahen Reservation,** called a First Nation Reserve in Canada. Each moment takes you deeper and deeper into rural and more forested areas. Nearly each person in Tofino had to take this same trip to arrive at the end of the highway. Just before travelers burst out onto the saltwater views, they pass through **Pacific Rim National Park.**

Arriving in Tofino, you may hear many foreign languages and notice numerous backpack-toting twenty-somethings speaking French, Dutch, German, and Italian. Do not be put off by their dreadlocks and body piercings. They tend to be nice people who love to chat about all the subjects common to travelers.

Tofino does not just belong to the young. The city-style prices at motels and restaurants tell you that most of the visitors are well-to-do families and couples. Despite the wide range of ages and incomes of Tofino's guests, all visitors are united in our joy of the outdoors. The principal activities for tourists include gazing at the forest-rock-sea vistas that surround the village, as well as eating terrific meals at pricey restaurants. Most people come to Tofino for active recreation, like walking the sandy beaches, kayaking, fishing, whale watching, scuba, surfing, bird watching, or hiking. Dress is casual and sporty. Motorcycle tourists are such obvious outdoor lovers; we fit in just fine.

This fruit stand is one of the last signs of civilization on the way to Tofino. In a few miles, it will be back country paved highway.

Once a logging road cut into the wilderness, the paved roads near Tofino can thrill a biker.

On our last visit, we booked a kayak tour of the islands around Tofino. It's eerie how, in just a few moments, a paddler can be eons away from civilization among ancient forests and floating on a secret-filled sea. The island-sheltered waters are often glassy and easy to paddle.

My farseeing wife always reserves a bed-and-breakfast six months before our departure to busy Tofino. Despite the whole town being full of B&Bs, as well as modest and pretentious motels, on our last visit, there was not a room to be had. The other village in the area, **Ucluelet,** was also booked.

I don't like to hike in my motorcycle boots, and often space is so limited, I can't pack a solid pair of sneakers. As a result, I often miss some nice hikes on my travels. Since my wife will not cave in to my boot excuse, I always try to cram in sneakers when traveling with Sharon, and I'm so glad I did on our last trip. There's a hike in Ucluelet called **The Wild Pacific Trail** that I'd do even in motorcycle boots. It's a new trail through woods and along the craggy coast. Even the birds find the trail so new, they flit unafraid past hikers. When you stop at the visitors center near the national park, they'll give you a free map of this and other hikes.

The forests often seem as if a human has never stepped foot in them before.

Americans have Crater Lake National Park. Canadians have **Pacific Rim National Park Reserve.** All 114 sites were full. Rangers were sending would-be campers to a parking lot that they use for overflow. Other visitors were taking the three-hour drive back to the town of **Port Alberni.** Book ahead! If you make an unplanned visit to Tofino, the visitor center just outside the national park has a staff that knows what rooms on the peninsula might be available and will book you on the spot. Arrive early.

If you are on a budget, get a place with a kitchen and cook for yourself. Tofino has a nice grocery and liquor store. You can buy salmon, crab, bread, wine, and salad to have a picnic on the beach or your motel balcony. For us, this beats nearly any dinner out at a fancy restaurant.

Still, if you get to the **Long Beach Lodge Resort** early enough to grab a sea-facing seat at their restaurant, a slow meal watching the sunset over **Long Beach** is a treasure. If you like boutique meals, the **Café Pamplona** offers views of the **Botanical Garden** while you eat beautifully presented meals.

No matter what rings your bell gastronomically, you should have lunch or dinner at **Sobos.** You might wonder that I recommend this place since it is just food from a purple deli truck parked a block away from the main highway (on an annoyingly bad gravel road). You eat your meal at picnic tables surrounded by all levels of society. Ahh, the food. As soon as you bite into your fish taco or smoked oyster packet, you will understand my recommendation and tell your friends.

Sobos can be hard to find. As you enter Tofino, you will pass **Beach Grocery** and **Live to Surf.** Back behind these businesses, Sobos waits to give you a terrific and reasonably priced meal.

To get to Sobos, the national park, and Tofino, you need to travel the worst paved road I've ever ridden. Years ago loggers built roads into the deep forests of Vancouver Island. When they encountered a gully, they filled it with stumps, log ends, rocks, and finally gravel. Anything in order to get the timber to the mill. Often the road winds more than necessary in order to access rich stands of trees. Later, this road was paved and voila!: a perfect motorcycle road twisting through forest, lake, and sea view areas.

This sea plane taxies into the wind before a noisy takeoff. The dock is not a place of peace.

CHAPTER 3

Obstacle Avoidance

A positive aspect of this bad road is a chance to hone your obstacle avoidance skills. Treat the rough parts of the road like you would an accidental view of your mother's underpants: don't look directly at them. Instead, look at your path around the problem. Due to a human condition called Target Fixation, bikers who stare at a spot on the pavement tend to hit it. Bikers who fix on a safe path around the obstacle, viewing the bad part only with peripheral vision, tend to keep their bike on the safe track. Never look directly at an obstruction! You can practice this at home by laying out a track in a parking lot, then placing small stuffed animals in the path. When you negotiate the route, always look for your path around the stuffed animals.

Notice the Native canoes at the base of this dock. Just 60 miles south of here, Natives still hunt whales in boats like these.

CHAPTER

3

On nearly all the thousands of tiny islands along the west coast of Vancouver Island, trees provide shelter for abundant sea birds.

What about all those stumps decaying under the pavement? As they compacted, the road sank in places. Maintenance crews, existing on shoe-string budgets, can not keep up with the sink holes. Most of the really bad places are marked with lower speed limits, but some are not. The curves may tempt you to get some serious lean angles, but the sunken grades—often lurking behind blind turns—compel you to ride with caution. My suggestion is to ride slow and keep your eyes on the road. Use the pullouts to let other vacationers pass you and give you a chance to stare at the natural wonders. Vacationers don't care if they bottom out their rental cars' springs.

The road starting 25 miles west of Port Alberni can be a fun and safe journey. Macho bikers who can't let themselves be passed by anyone might ruin their bike or body. Let them pass you. You will make it safely to Tofino.

Tofino. Since its location makes it lonely and romantic—since its food, ambiance and views make it desirable—since its popularity makes it more desirable, Tofino remains a place that's hard to reach, hard to stay in, and hard to leave.

CHAPTER

3

Trip 9 British Columbia Sisters: Whistler & Lillooet

Distance *160 miles (4.5 hours)*

Terrain *Nearly all roads in British Columbia are slow. This is due to speed limits, road conditions, and traffic. Give yourself plenty of time to get anywhere. Most of the roads on this journey are two-lane rural highways. Watch for rocks near cliffs and forest animals.*

Highlights *Changing colors on Howe Sound, cliff hugging roads, deep forests, alpine lakes, urbane charm of Whistler Village, enormous mountain-sized rocks, and glaciers on Duffy Lake Road*

The Duffy Lake Road north of Pemberton often seems devoid of traffic and heavily populated with breathtaking scenery.

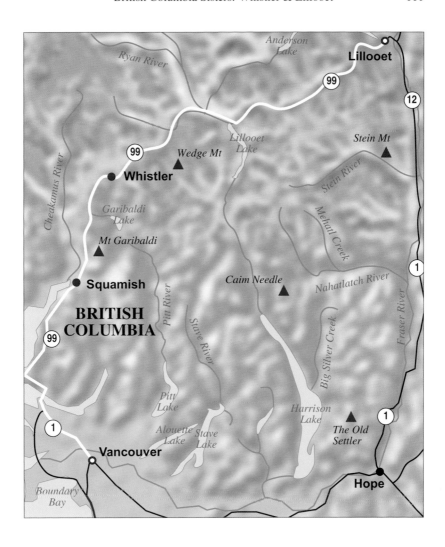

The Route From Vancouver

0   From Vancouver, go west on Canada 1. This will become 99

43   Arrive in Squamish. Continue north on 99

80   Arrive in Whistler. Continue north on 99

158 Arrive in Lillooet

CHAPTER

3

These bikers enjoy the curves near Duffy Lake. Watch for some sunken pavement in this area.

Have you ever tasted a wild strawberry? The fruit, about the size of a red vitamin pill, has all the essence of a big berry concentrated into an intense tart tablet. This describes the road between **Vancouver** and **Lillooet**—the essence of British Columbia in one tart ride.

Much of this journey is called the **Sea to Sky Highway,** since it begins at the saltwater/rainforest area called **Howe Sound** and runs north along **Garibaldi Provincial Park.** Here, mountain lakes and mixed fir forests live their quiet lives. Suddenly, in the midst of all this raw wilderness rises the worldly resort town of **Whistler.** Continuing north on a former Indian trail, you will enter an area of wild forest, sharp mountains, and deep stream-filled canyons. Long sinuous waterfalls call from across vast canyons, their cries echoed in hidden streams.

Oddly, here in soggy British Columbia, the land becomes more arid and even sagebrush appears as you approach Lillooet. In a small, 160-mile tablet, a biker can sample nearly the whole flavor of British Columbia. Rainforest to desert, sea to mountain, rural to urban.

CHAPTER

3

The area of British Columbia totals an astounding 364,764 square miles. This is greater than twice the area of Oregon and Washington combined. Packed into this huge space are four major mountain ranges, a gigantic coastline, sophisticated cities, and fantastic motorcycle rides.

You might think flannel-shirted hockey fans populate the whole great province. It turns out this beautiful province has a widely varied population, with the top five languages being English, Chinese, Punjabi, German, and French. Fleece is more common than flannel.

Enough background information. You want to try this ride, right? Begin this sample of western British Columbia from Vancouver by heading west on Canada Highway 1. After about 10 miles, this turns into 99 near **Horseshoe Bay.** Like clockwork, the winds pick up in the afternoons, so a morning trip will offer a more comfortable ride.

I believe this early section of Highway 99 could be one of the most perfect motorcycle roads I've ever ridden, if it weren't for the traffic. Beautiful curves cut into the cliffs, scenic views of Howe Sound, temperate rainforests, snow covered mountains, good pavement, and revealed apexes make this road special. During the summer, thousands of tourists embark on this cliff-hugging passage. Trucks carrying tourist-nurturing supplies take the same route.

On weekends, you can feel as if you are in a long line of traffic stretching from Horseshoe Bay to Whistler. The advantage of the 25 to 45 mph pace is a chance for a biker to catch views of blue green forests and deep blue waters. As you motor up the Sound, the waters gradually morph into glacial-silt green, becoming milkier as you proceed north. Despite the infrequent pullouts along the early part of 99 (don't cross a double yellow line to get to a pullout), your mind can satisfy that special hunger with these precious wild scenes.

In British Columbia, many of these wild scenes involve the air and water. Everything is so vast, you see more atmosphere. If the sky is not a perfect shade of pure blue, you may get to see lacy tendrils of cloud cling to the forest tops. If you are riding in morning or evening, the water becomes a pewter sheet and the forest scents hang in the air. This is British Columbia.

About 45 miles from Vancouver, you arrive in **Squamish.** An enormous orb of solid granite, shaped like an upside down strawberry, it serves as a magnet to rock climbers, and dominates the town of Squamish. Take a number if you want to climb **"The Chief."** Squamish supplies thousands of climbers and travelers with fast food, gas, and clean motels. I suggest a light lunch just south of town at the simple **Britiana Beach Coffee House** near

These rock-solid mountains can rise up dramatically in front of you. Keep your camera ready.

the mining museum. If you want something hardy, the rock climbers favor the **Howe Sound Inn and Brewery** in downtown Squamish.

Continuing out of Squamish, you leave the sound, stained green by glacial deposits, and enter a wild forest and lake area. Still you are in line with the rest of the traffic. As you approach Whistler, you may notice the traffic moving faster and signs of civilization as you pass the innocent lakes near town.

Whistler started out as a small fly fishing lodge on **Alta Lake** back in 1914. Now it has become a cosmopolitan and posh ski and summer resort. Like the successful sister, nonchalantly wearing her gaudy jewels, the resort town of Whistler stands ready to dazzle the traveler.

Town planners got it right. If you book a hotel near "the village," you can park your bike in an underground, card-lock garage and see the sights on foot. Most of "the village" is a pedestrian zone packed with fancy designer shops from which goods pour out into the happy hands of well-dressed shoppers. The result is a feeling that you are living in a theme park.

Neither my wife nor I are shoppers, but we love savoring an ice cream cone while watching people. If you are on a budget, book a room with a kitchen and prepare your own meals and picnics. Restaurants are plentiful and often pricey, yet just a short walk away you can find yourself picnicking at **Lost Lake,** looking up at the snow streaked mountains. Bring your swimsuit.

Up the road 80 miles, this great lady's older sister wears a shabby dress that was once the prettiest in town. **Lillooet** (rhymes with cigarette), once a booming gold rush town with a population of 20,000, faded as the gold dust petered out and is now recovering. Mining remains the economic engine of this dessert oasis, but tourism is starting to make the lady sit up proudly again. Its population is nearly 2,000. Pretend you don't notice the row of dilapidated trailers outside of town.

The woods hide secrets that binoculars can reveal. Toss in a pair before leaving on this trip.

Renting Bikes in Canada

I love riding Harleys. In Oregon, it's the only bike available for rent. Due to reasonable insurance rates, things are different in Canada. You can rent beautiful Harleys, but the renting menu is much richer here. Below are the contact numbers for some rental places in British Columbia. When you call, be sure to find out about requirements, additional charges, gear provided or available for rent, transportation from the airport, and so forth. Keep aware of the riding seasons in various places in Canada. Many of these rental places offer guided tours.

Coastline Motorcycle Adventure Tours
(866) 338-0344
www.coastlinemc.com
(Harley-Davidsons only)

Cycle BC Rentals
(866) 380-2453
www.cyclebc.ca
(Rents sport, touring, and cruiser motorcycles from Vancouver and Victoria, British Columbia)

The Great Canadian Motor Corporation
(800) 667-8865
www.gcmc.com
(Rents: Honda, Harley-Davidson, BMW, Yamaha, Suzuki, and Kawasaki sport-touring, cruiser, and dual-sport motorcycles)

McScoot's Motorcycle and Scooter Rentals Kelowna
(250) 766-5442 (Oct 1–April 30)
(250) 763-4668 (May 1–Sept 30)
www.mcscoots.com
(Harley-Davidson only)

Pacific Motorcycle Adventure Tours & Rentals Inc.
(604) 883-9842
(877) 883-9842
www.pacificmotorcycle.com
(Honda, BMW, Kawasaki, and Suzuki dual-sport, cruiser, and sport-touring models)

Mineral deposits stain the otherwise perfect gray mountains near Joffre Lake Park.

Connecting these two sisters winds a mountain highway sometimes called Duffy Lake Road. Most maps label this Highway 99. From Whistler to Lillooet, traffic thins out. Watch for rocks, deer, and slow moving vehicles around blind turns on the 15 percent grades. You may encounter sunken pavement near **Seton Lake** a few miles south of Lillooet. Often you round a bend and are hit in the eye with an expansive and stunning view of mountains, cliffs, and valleys. Intense beauty! Delicious!

Along **Duffy Lake Road,** wild flowers grow lustily, while up on the mountains, glaciers glow like benign atomic-powered blue-white glass. Despite the sparse traffic, you will stop just to stare. **Joffre Lake Provincial Park** makes a good glacier-viewing rest stop. If the valley was hot, this place will be cool and refreshing. Ahead waits British Columbia's only desert.

Just a mile from Lillooet, **Naxwit Rest Area** offers green shady grass for napping, picnic tables, clean pit toilets, and displays interpreting the area.

Like the intense tart, sweet taste of a wild strawberry, the roads, vistas, and towns of this ride beg to be sampled again. You might wonder that this whole journey is only 160 miles. I view this trip as a pail of wild strawberries to be eaten slowly, one at a time, not mindlessly devoured. Pause at the towns, rest areas, and pullouts to savor the sharp-sweet flavors of British Columbia.

From Lillooet, you can connect to the trip through **Hope** (Trip 7) or resample the strong flavors of these same roads going back to Vancouver.

Some Canadians consider this part of Duffy Lake Road to be the best biking road in British Columbia.

Squamish Food

Howe Sound Inn & Brewing Company
(800) 919-2537
www.howesound.com

The Coffee Break
40330 Tantalus Way
(604) 898-5011

Whistler Lodging

http://whistlerblackcomb.com
(888) 858-4845
(Ask for prices printed in their vacation guide)

Lillooet Lodging

Four Pines Motel
(800) 753-2576
www.4pinesmotel.com
(Ask for one of the newer rooms)

Olexson Esso
(250) 256-4456
lolexson@telus.net
(Bed and breakfast)

Lillooet Food

Breakfast and lunch: Lou's

Dinner: Dina's

Picnic: Naxwit Rest stop just south of town

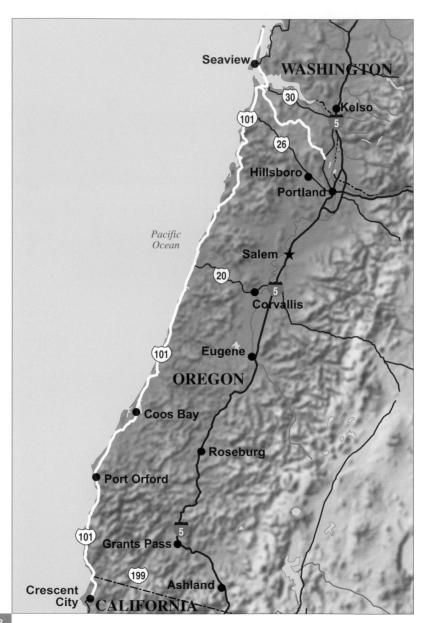

A Coastal Journey

The Pacific Northwest coast provided the native populations with a rich and dependable source of food. These natives were so wealthy that they had the time to create some of the finest native art on the North American continent. The technological advances, their robust economy, and their culture affected life for early Americans west of the Rockies from Cape Mendocino to southeast Alaska. Today the coastal regions continue to embody an economic engine that powers much of the modern culture and economy of the Pacific Northwest.

I took a friend of mine from Germany to the beach and his first comment was: Where are all the people? Despite the power and beauty of this region, it remains a place where a person can find a surf-pounding stillness—larger than alone.

Since the beaches are a tourist draw, lively arts festivals, bouncing bars, lonely lighthouses, fascinating historical sites and terrific restaurants are more common than unbroken sand dollars.

Sand dunes drift over the highway near Florence. Sand is usually not a driving hazard for bikes that remain on the road.

Most of Long Beach Peninsula is so flat, the community has made plans to deal with a gigantic wave.

The natives traded dentalium shells, elk hide armor, slaves, and food; modern coastal businesses provide support for travelers, a lively fishery, and sports fishing. It's easy to spend a day shopping, hiking, fishing, and eating in many of the pretty coastal towns that dot the coast.

One of my favorite activities is to stop at one of the hundreds of pullouts along side the great Highway 101. From these special spots you can feel the salt wind in your face, listen to the briny crash of the waves, and feel the swell of enormous wildness in your chest. Short hikes can take you to secret places that may be haunted by ghosts of natives raking clams, harvesting mussels, or tending fish traps.

From these pullouts, the blue ocean, punctuated by rocky outcroppings, shelters one of the most biologically diverse places on earth. If you take the time to stare into a tide pool, hundreds of creatures and plants will reveal themselves to you. Nearly every evening you can get a sunset photo that will make your friends want to follow you back to that spot.

If I were living in a hot place far from the Oregon Coast, I'd consider renting a nice bike and taking this coastal trip. On page 132, you can find out how to rent in order to make an escape to a cool and beautiful place. While your friends are running from air conditioned car to air conditioned building, you can be outside in a cool, fresh, clean place where you keep your vents closed for most of the ride. In the evening, you can sit outside your motel and watch the sea offer wave after wave to the sandy shores, your chest full of pity for anyone not with you.

For people who are unfamiliar with Pacific North Coast delicacies, I always recommend trying the **Dungeness crab.** It's light, flaky meat that is frustratingly difficult to extract from the shell. If you pick up a whole crab, a loaf of bread, wine and salad, you can sip the wine while using the pliers from your tool kit to open the crab shells. Every sea food restaurant sells it mixed in with just about anything you can think of from pasta to meat loaf, but the flavor is so delicate, I prefer it with salad.

If your waistline permits you to eat fried foods, find a restaurant that offers fresh **razor clams.** Cooked properly, they are firm, tender and embody the flavor of the Pacific North Coast.

As a child, I constantly dreamed of the coast. As an adult, I look back to see how important it's been to my family and friends. Like the early natives, I feel wealthy to have this area available for biking, dreaming, and eating.

California redwoods near Crescent City are a must see. Nothing on earth compares to the feeling of these precious groves.

CHAPTER

4

Trip 10   Oregon Coast Bedtime Story

Distance   *370 miles without side trips (two day ride with stops)*

Terrain   *Curvy, mostly sweeping roads, somewhat congested at north end of the coast. Hazards include deer, RVs driven by renters, distracting views*

Highlights   *Cool climate, lonely rocky vistas, deserted expansive beaches, ocean sunsets, and great seafood*

This story began long ago in a hot, dusty town in northern California. My brother and I would lie awake in our bunk beds and plan our way out of the heat. We'd get a couple of motorcycles and blast out of the simmering California valley to make our way to the cool, green Oregon Coast. Just him and me.

Instead, we grew up to escape the heat in different ways, Roger put down roots south of San Francisco, and I moved to Oregon. Families, jobs, and reality long kept us from this coastal ride. Finally, we recently completed our cool beachside ride. This is the story of how you can experience your own Oregon Coast story.

The pavement on Highway 101 along the Oregon Coast tends to be in top condition all summer.

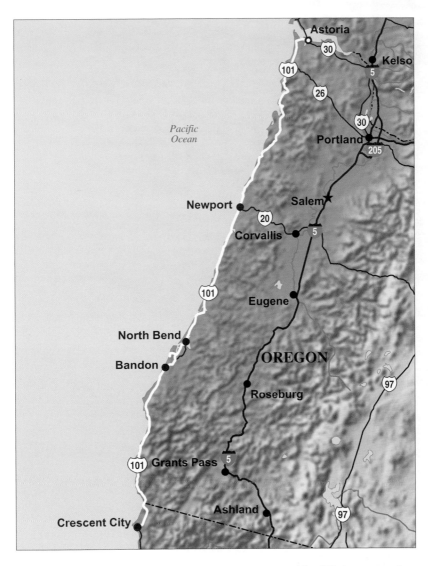

When we were kids, our destination was nonspecific. We just wanted to be at a beach that was not hot. In truth, the wild and scenic **Oregon Coast** offers much more than relief from heat. In 1967 the Oregon Legislature adopted the **Oregon Beach Bill** that made all beaches in Oregon public property. The whole coast is publicly owned. You can walk on any beach you please. No other state has had the kahunas to stare wealthy landowners in the eye and make them share their beaches. As a result, a biker's destination is not one certain beach, but all precious 400 miles of State Highway 101.

CHAPTER

4

The Route From Astoria

0   From Astoria, go south on Highway 101

231   Turn right onto Newmark about one mile past North Bend. You are following the signs to Sunset Bay/Cape Arago State Parks

235   Turn left to stay on Cape Arago Highway. Continue to follow any signs to Cape Arago

253   Pause at Cape Arago for photos. Retrace your way back the way you came

257   After about four miles, look for the signs to Bandon. This road is called Seven Devils Road. It will change names to Beaver Hill Road after about six miles

270   Turn south onto 101

379   Arrive in Crescent City. Explore the redwoods at this point!

Astoria has a great Maritime Museum. You can tour the Columbia River Lightship as part of your admission price.

CHAPTER

4

Astorians are proud of their newly restored Astor Column. High above the town, this makes a terrific viewpoint.

Along the way you can pause at hundreds of turnouts and more state and local parks per mile than any place in America. The sparsely populated southern part of Oregon shows off naked sandy stretches of pristine sand. Each walk on these beaches yields up some sort of treasure: a shell, an agate, a fossil. Other solitary coastal views show scattered rocks emerging from the surf like an army of sea gods preparing to attack the shores. Wind sculpted trees shelter sweet, fragile ferns and other coastal plants that tell a visitor that this place is different.

Roger flew up from San Francisco and rented a red touring bike. We packed his bike and took off on a rural back road, State Highway 202, from **Portland** to **Astoria.**

CHAPTER

4

Heceta Head lighthouse is far too pretty for a quick glance through a face shield.

Astoria is like a homely younger sister who wakes up one day to find herself beautiful. She doesn't quite know what to do with her beauty. The old Victorian homes awkwardly show off their newly restored charm, the old town proudly wears its 1950s character; the shops, restaurants, and waterfront pull in tourists like magnets. The fishing trawlers and charter boats still go about the business of fishing. Just a few years ago, the town seemed shabby, neglected and suffering from some kind of sea rot. Now it's undergoing an energetic economic boom. Civic pride, like the sea breezes, refreshed Roger and me. We wanted to linger, but Highway 101 called us to continue.

Given the call of the road, you might think we would make rapid progress down the coast. The Oregon Coast has so many view points, parks, pull-outs, light houses, pretty coastal towns, and other distractions, the point of riding this unique beach highway becomes sampling the varied treats at 101's smorgasbord, not just heading for the roast beef and a table.

Some of these treats include the tiny town of **Cannon Beach.** Pick up an ice cream cone and browse the interesting shops and galleries. With over 400,000 visitors a year, this little town is set up for tourists. The massive basalt stone monolith near town, **Haystack Rock,** shelters hundreds of sea birds and marine tidal creatures. The town will fine you $1,500 if you climb on it, so just take pictures.

CHAPTER

4

I could never understand why the **Tillamook Cheese Factory** is such a big tourist draw. Roger had to stop, so we took the tour. They do have great ice cream (and cheese), but I wanted to put my bike back on 101. Since Roger is the older brother, and new to the Oregon Coast, he usually gets his way.

We parked the bikes again at **Depot Bay.** The shops beckon travelers, but be sure to watch the boats struggle with the narrow opening from the shelter of the world's smallest harbor. We watched during a slack tide, but I've watched boats thrown back by the crashing waves and violent tidal currents. Exciting!

Another stop I recommend is **Newport.** Besides being awash with traditional tourist activities, including a wax museum and a great coastal aquarium, you need to stroll the docks. Commercial fishermen bring in their catch for processing right next to fishing charters. Many claim that **Mo's Restaurant** serves the best clam chowder in the world. For a great breakfast or dinner you can also try **The Whale's Tale.**

Near Bandon, the Coquille River Lighthouse was built in 1896 to guide ships across the treacherous bar at the mouth of the river.

CHAPTER
4

Make your way to the old town part of Newport for great food, views of working fishing boats, and the famous bridge.

Our first night we spent at **Florence.** This pretty town is about half way down the coast. My personal rules for finding a motel on the coast are: avoid the Shilo Inn-type chains, be off the road by 3:00 p.m. on a weekend or holiday, and avoid the heaviest tourists areas. Many bikers camp in one of the 50 coastal campgrounds, but I prefer a clean, cheap strip motel with my bike parked 10 feet from my window. From Florence, 50 miles of amazing sand dunes draw thousands of visitors and their sand toys.

Just north of Florence lies one of the most photographed views in Oregon: **Heceta** (heh SEE tah) **Head Lighthouse.** The collision of the blue-green ocean, browny blacks of the basalt rocks, and whitewashed red-roofed 19th century lighthouse compel a viewer to gaze far too long. In addition, the twisting highway on this part of the coast was cut into the hard rock cliff as if the engineer loved motorcycles himself.

Many coastal travelers miss **Cape Arago State Park** when they travel 101. Approaching this special place from the north, a biker must motor through about 30–40 minutes of rather slow suburban traffic in low-income areas of the town of **Coos Bay.** To get to Cape Arago, follow the signs to State Parks/Charleston. The delay is worth it for the views and natural coastal forest.

CHAPTER

4

Another reason to visit Cape Arago is the trip from the cape to **Bandon.** Going south, after you leave Cape Arago, watch for the sign to Bandon (Seven Devils Road). Due to the ugly clear cuts along this road, the turns are mostly laid bare. Light traffic and quality pavement make this a wonder road for bikers who enjoy sinuous roads taken at moderate speeds. If you are coming from the south, catch this roller coaster road by looking for the signs to **Charleston** about nine miles north of Bandon (called Beaver Hill/Seven Devils Road on this side).

Ancient, old growth coastal forests offer a silent wildness that makes a visitor linger and return.

CHAPTER

4

Renting Bikes In Portland

A visitor can rent Harleys from two different places in the Portland area: Latus Motors and Paradise Harley. A renter must be 25 years old or more, possess a valid motorcycle license, and have proper motorcycle gear (DOT approved helmet). We always buy the collision damage wavier, but you can check with your insurance or credit card company to see if they cover this for you. Call or visit the websites to get more information. In Oregon, it's only possible to rent Harleys.

Latus Motors
(503) 249-8653
(800) 446-2525
www.latus-hd.com

Paradise Harley
(503) 924-3700
www.paradiseh-d.com

No special gear is needed to ride the coast—except rain protection. I like to take my fabric jacket since it's waterproof, warm, and converts to a mesh jacket in the heat. Roger, never a light packer, can't climb on his bike without wearing his leathers and his rainsuit packed in the duffle.

An inexpensive motel with a great location is **Shoreline Motel** in **Port Orford.** The ocean view is to die for and it's right next to a fabulous restaurant called **The Breadworks.**

We never seemed to get tired of checking out the lighthouses along the way. As children, we never gave much thought to lighthouses, but when you actually see them, they form a fantasy point for a lonely life of bringing order to chaos. Maybe when we grow up, Roger and I will be lighthouse keepers and shine our light into the void to help travelers.

Often people find the southern coast to be their favorite part of the trip. While some of the north coast towns pretend to be sophisticated, the south coast towns seem simple, honest, and happy with who they are. In addition, the beaches show their beauty openly, unashamed, for all to see. Yet few footprints can be found. It's as if travelers are rushing to the north and missing some of the best parts, or perhaps these beaches refuse to be disturbed.

I suggest a stop in Bandon. Largely due to the presence of a world-class golf course, **Bandon Dunes,** the economy of this sleepy coast town has been on the upswing. They've constructed a wonderful system of public docks and walkways. You can stroll along, view the public art, and chat with people fishing and tending crab traps.

We ended our coastal trip by passing into a redwood grove on the California side. Those rusty giants of the earth never cease to stir emotions in me. The deepest words cannot describe their power and beauty.

Both Roger and I agreed we had the right idea when we made our bunk-bed plans for an Oregon Coast tour. We couldn't agree what part we liked the best: the clean and lonely beaches, the terrible power of the ocean, or the feeling of motorcycling cool, winding roads. We lay on our queen-sized mattresses that last night planning to repeat this trip.

Newport Food

The Whale's Tale
(541) 265-8660

Mo's Restaurant
(541) 265-7512

Port Orford Food and Lodging

Shoreline Motel
(541) 332-2903

Port Orford Breadworks
(541) 332-4022

Goldbeach Food and Lodging

Indian Creek Café
(541) 247-0680
(Follow the Rogue River along the south side for a mile from town)

CHAPTER
4

Trip 11   Portland to Long Beach Loop

Distance   *252 miles (I suggest two days. Spend the night in the Long Beach area so you don't miss the sunset)*

Terrain   *Considering you are riding around the mouth of one of the mightiest rivers on the continent and the longest white sand beach in the world, this ride is remarkably curvy. Watch for poor pavement east of Astoria, deer, and tourist traffic.*

Highlights   *Pleasant, rural roads, forest hallways, Victorian charm in Astoria and Oysterville, salty white beach views and sunsets, great food*

Some summers you just want a cool, friendly ride to a pretty place. You want to eat some great food, watch a sunset, browse some shops, and take a moonlight walk on a long, sandy beach. According to locals, you can do all this on the longest sandy beach in the world. No, it's not Cox's Bazar on the Bay of Bengal, it's the aptly named peninsula of **Long Beach, Washington.**

If you approach this from **Portland, Oregon** to the south, there's a secret road I want to tell you about. You are probably thinking that I'm going to tell you to take Highway 30 from Portland to **Astoria.** After all, if you look at a map, you can see little dots along that route. Little dots make my heart beat fast with anticipation—a scenic highway.

Is it really the longest beach? I'm not sure, but I never grow tired of it.

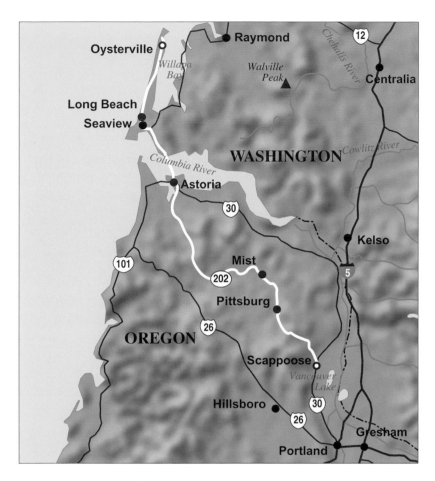

Since 1792, when Captain Robert Gray sailed his ship, The Columbia, into the great river of the west, this gigantic waterway has ceased being a secret. As a result, Highway 30 is an often congested, sometimes stop-and-go ride, which moves along with hundreds of other travelers. I'm not saying it's unpleasant, but it's not my kind of ride.

I like an untamed ride, far from traffic and congestion. To take my secret road, you need to make your way to **Scappoose, Oregon.** This little mill town is only about 15 miles west of Portland on Highway 30. Instead of staying on 30 to Astoria, you are going to turn left just outside of Scappoose toward **Vernonia.** The road immediately starts to take you up, away from the Columbia. You'll pass by rural homes and watch the cool waters of **Scappoose Creek** tumble over rocks. As the homes quickly thin out, you will see some small farms and timbered hills.

CHAPTER

4

The Route From Scapoose

Find this town just west of Portland on Highway 30

0   Leave Scappoose going west on Highway 30

1   Turn left following the signs to Vernonia/Pittsburg

21   Turn right at the Hwy 47/Hwy 202 junction going toward Mist

77   As you enter Astoria, work your way downtown and look for signs to the Astor Column

79   From the Astor Column, go back down the hill toward the waterfront. Turn left (south on Marine Drive)

81   Follow the signs to Highway 101 north/Astoria Bridge. Cross the bridge and follow the signs to Long Beach/Illwaco

111   Arrive in Oysterville

The Route From Oysterville to Scappoose

0   Leave Oysterville going south on 103

15   Turn north onto 101

28   Turn south onto Highway 4 going toward Longview

81   Outside Longview, turn right onto Highway 432

86   Follow signs to Highway 30/Oregon. Cross the Lewis and Clark Bridge

87   Turn east onto Highway 30 toward St. Helens

115   Arrive in Scappoose

The road gains energy and twists through mixed forests and hallways of trees. Bursting out into a clear cut, you can suddenly see many of the turns ahead. The hazards on this road include some uneven pavement, rare bits of gravel on the road, and persistent log trucks on weekdays.

Almost exactly 20 miles after leaving Scappoose, you come to the Highway 47 junction. Turn right toward **Mist.** If you packed a picnic or need a break, you will come across **Big Eddy County Park** 10 miles later. It's free to use the park if you stay less than 20 minutes.

I love this road, which parallels the winding **Nehalem River.** You pass through tiny towns like **Natal** with its 90-year-old schoolhouse and Grange hall, **Birkenfeld** with a historic store, and **The Country Museum** with its 8-foot-diameter log and **Peterson House Museum.** The town of Mist has its store—the oldest continuously operating business in Oregon, with great sandwiches and milkshakes. In Mist, you follow 202 west toward Astoria. Don't take 47 north to **Clatskanie.** It's a fun road, but it puts you back on busy Highway 30.

In **Jewell,** you really need to look for the elk herd. Sometimes you can see a 100 of these half-ton beasts munching the grass with no apparent concern for tourists. If you have loud pipes, try to lug your engine a bit so you (and others) can get a peek or a photograph of these magnificent animals.

There is a 20-mile lonely reach of highway between Jewell and **Olney.** The pavement becomes rough toward the end of this stretch. Watch for potholes and cracks. Go slow.

The Oysterville Church has brochures inside detailing a walking tour of this quaint town.

CHAPTER

4

Oysterville boasts huge piles of oyster shells near the bay.

After you pass the old store at the town of Olney, you will notice that you seem to be on the outskirts of a big town.

Astoria. Locals like to claim it was founded in 1811, but it wasn't until 1860 that it really began to boom. By the turn of the century, Astoria was Oregon's second largest city. Affluent, gentile, and bawdy, the city pulsed with sailors, loggers, and fishermen mixing with parasol, lace-handkerchief ladies and top-hat gentlemen.

A center for shipping, fishing, and trade, there remains ample evidence of its former prosperity. Like the stubble on an old fisherman's chin, the steep hillsides prickle with beautifully restored Victorian homes. You can tour one of the most ornate, **The Flavel House.** Built by Captain George Flavel in the 1885, it allowed the distinguished gentleman to keep an eye on his ships from his home.

Bikers love the view from the recently restored **Astoria Column** with its expansive views of Astoria, the **Columbia River,** the Pacific Ocean, and points east. You need to buy a parking permit to stop and take pictures. Expect to see deer.

From Astoria, you are going to travel the 4-mile-long **Astoria Bridge,** the longest truss bridge in the world. Once you arrive in Washington, turn left (east) toward **Long Beach** on Highway 401. If time permits, you can explore **Fort Canby State Park,** with its 27 miles of ocean beach and two lighthouses. Otherwise, keep following the signs to Long Beach.

With 28 miles of beautiful beaches, this is truly a long beach. Sadly, crass commercialization, t-shirt shops, and fast food spots have removed much of the charm of this area in the towns of Long Beach and **Seaview.** Still, our favorite restaurants, nearly across the street from each other, are the **42nd Street Restaurant** and **Laurie's Homestead Breakfast House.** These are right on the main drag in Seaview.

I know it's cheesy, but I really enjoy spending an hour in **Marsh's Free Museum.** Back in 1921, Bill Marsh displayed a varied collection of odd artifacts, including a two-headed calf, old toys and musical instruments, glass fishing floats, a real-live (well maybe not living) shrunken head, and Jake the Alligator Man. Jake is a mummified creature that is half man/half alligator.

The Grays River Covered bridge is the last working covered bridge in Washington. (Photo by Sharon Hansen)

CHAPTER
4

It's just sand, but the ever-changing patterns on the surface entertain beachcombers.

The first time we visited this area, we noticed a sign for a cranberry museum. What would they put in a cranberry museum? After seeing the alligator man, I pictured a cranberry in the shape of Richard Nixon or a 42-pound giant cranberry. Instead we learned how this tart fruit is grown and harvested. If you want something made from cranberry, the gift shop probably has it.

After leaving the carnival atmosphere of Long Beach, you'll see a huge contrast in **Oysterville** on the bay side of the **Long Beach Peninsula.** This place is so quaint and charming in an 1880s way, the whole town was put on the National Register of Historic Places back in 1976. A booming oyster business brought a surge of prosperity to this little town. Stop by the **Oysterville Church** and pick up a walking tour brochure.

Looking at a map, you are going to want to head out to **Leadbetter Point State Park.** It's the end of the peninsula and a state park. If you are expecting an organized park with trails to the beach, you will be disappointed. There are a few random "trails" to the beach with warnings about thigh-deep swampy trails. Most visitors wander over to the bay side of the park to watch birds. The one-lane road out there is quite fun on a bike.

When it's time to leave Long Beach Peninsula, you might want to take the scenic route. At Seaview, turn north on Highway 101. This allows you to ride a wonderful road along **Willapa Bay** before turning back south to follow Highway 4, which traces the north side **Columbia River** past fishing and resort villages. You can go just a couple miles off Hwy. 4 to explore the only functioning covered bridge in Washington. Running through **Grays River Covered Bridge,** the smell of creosote and old wood should evoke a memory in you. Look for the signs three miles east of **Grays River.**

Longview has a pleasant neighborhood along the **Cowliz River,** but unless you want to relax in the pretty, shaded city park, I'm going to advise you to by-pass the town. As you approach Longview, look for Highway 432 to your right. This takes you through an industrial part of town, but it's a simple way to find the **Lewis and Clark Bridge.** You want to cross this bridge to take the rural approach to Portland. Otherwise, you might find yourself fighting urban freeway traffic. The signs pointing to Oregon Highway 30 are hard to find if you do not take this truck route.

On Long beach Peninsula, a biker can take his motorcycle down for the sunset. Avoid getting stuck in the soft sand.

CHAPTER

4

The old railroad trestle bridge near Vernonia makes you think you've gone back in time.

After crossing this tall bridge, follow 30 toward **St. Helens** and Scappoose. Scappoose connects you back to Portland.

I know not everyone taking this journey will want to come back to Portland. From Long Beach you may want to cling to your alligator-man, oyster, long-sandy-beach memories and run up north to take the Olympic Peninsula ride (Trip 15). That night you can floss with cranberry dental floss and remember the longest beach in the world.

Information

Long Beach Chamber of Commerce
(306) 642-2400
(800) 451-2542

Lodging

Moby Dick Hotel
(360) 665-4543
(800) 673-6145
www.mobydickhotel.com
(Clean but rickety bed and breakfast away from Long Beach on the right on the bay)

CHAPTER
4

Caswell's on the Bay
(888) 553-2319
www.caswellsinn.com
(Posh, newer bed and breakfast inn on the Pacific)

Sunset View Resort
(800) 272-9199
(A bit more upscale)

The Shaman Motel
(800) 753-3750
www.shamanmotel.com
(Simple and in the center of everything)

Food and Fun

Marsh's Free Museum
(360) 642-2188
www.marshsfreemuseum.com
(See the alligator man)

42nd Street Café
(360) 642-2323
www.42ndstreetcafe.com
(Everything expertly cooked by a terrific chef)

Laurie's Homestead Breakfast House
(360) 642-7171
(Simple, good food)

Dooger's Seafood and Grill
(360) 642-4224
(Ask if the razor clams are fresh—yum!)

CHAPTER
4

The Great National Park Tour

Do you remember when you were a kid and your dad drove past a carnival or amusement park? What caught your attention first? The big rides, right? "Daddy can we go?" You may have asked. Those big rides called to you.

The Pacific Northwest has four big rides: the National Parks. These precious places pull in local and foreign visitors like a carnival sucking in kids and their dads, and well they should. These parks hold some of the world's greatest natural scenic treasures.

Think about the **Olympic National Park.** It throbs with life from the northern end of the Olympic Peninsula. I'm guessing the dark and mysterious **Hoh Rain Forest** has more moss-covered ancient trees than any other place on earth—at least several are over 1,000 years old. The Pacific Beaches always seem deserted and the place to engage a special kind of wild aloneness. **Hurricane Ridge** offers a biker a gain of over 5,000 feet in altitude in only 17 miles. When it's dry, it is truly one of my favorite biking roads. There are no woods more virgin than these. No mountains more wild, and no coast less comfortable with civilization.

Olympic National Park has few roads, but many trails. This one from the top of Hurricane Ridge can be walked in motorcycle boots.

Several years ago I visited these woods on a summer car trip and witnessed the heaviest rainfall I've ever seen. We watched a group of motorcyclists plow through the wall of rain, comfortable in their state-of-the-art rain gear. Make sure you are ready for this trip before embarking upon it.

Crater Lake: the only national park in Oregon, it defines the word blue for me. The trip I have planned for you not only lets you see the place that has inspired and awed visitors since the time of the first Native American visitor, the indomitable William Steel and the modern visitors, this trip also lets you visit another wonder of volcanic origin: a glass mountain. This trip reflects the volcanic wonders of the Pacific Northwest and will remain a part of you long after you return to your ordinary home.

On the road to Paradise Lodge, a biker can see other peaks crowding around Mt. Rainier.

You will never in your life see anything like the life exploding on the Hall of Moss hike in the Hoh Rain Forest. (Photo by Roger Hansen)

When people visit **Mt. Rainier,** they go to see the great mountain and its attractive **Paradise Lodge.** They like the clear air, the hikes and views of the immaculate wilderness surrounding the park. If you make this trip, I suggest you take your camera for the wildflower shots you'll get. Your friends will not believe your stories.

Park four is the **North Cascade National Park,** part of a hard, 300-mile day. If you cannot stomach the thought of seeing seven European countries in just three days, then you should extend this trip a day and include some exploring. Another reason to make this two days is if the weather is harsh or you are fatigued. When I travel this North Cascade National Park ride, the sheer, wild **Skagit River Canyon** gives me energy. The green waters seem to glow with a power that transfers to bikers, hikers, and other outdoor travelers.

These four big rides in the park draw travelers from all over the world. After you see these wonders, you will understand the magnetic pull of these big rides to the daddies who ride them.

CHAPTER

5

Trip 12 Seattle to Mt. Rainier

Distance *190 miles one way (all day)*

Terrain *Pleasant curving roads along rural highways, some choppy pavement in the national park, a few very tight turns winding up to the lodge*

Highlights *Snoqualmie Falls, rural scenes, deep forests, clear streams, mountain wildflowers, tall trees swaying in the breeze, grand old Paradise Lodge*

This Indian Paintbrush is typical of the flowers that follow the thaw up the mountain. At any time of the summer, a visitor can find wild flowers on Mt. Rainier.

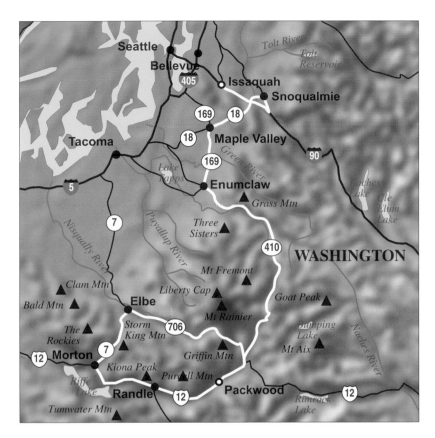

Why start a ride to the highest point in Washington in a town like **Issaquah?** You might think it's because Seattleites consider this town out in the country. Who wants to ride around in the city? It could be the availability of outstanding rental bikes (see renting in Washington page 155). Perhaps it's the name of the town itself—it's fun to say Issaquah (ISS ah quah).

Whatever the reason, I suggest you begin your trip by pulling out of Issaquah and going right for **Snoqualmie Falls.** You will get on Interstate 90 toward **Spokane,** but take the Highway 18 exit (number 25) toward the Snoqualmie Parkway. If this sounds complicated, don't worry. There are plenty of signs pointing the way to Snoqualmie Falls.

Turn left onto 18 and follow the signs toward the falls. From the viewing platform, you can watch the waters of **Snoqualmie River** tumble 270 feet down into the canyon. Knowing I'm going to be staying at simple strip motels for a few days, I also like to wander into the posh **Snoqualmie Lodge** and include it in my fantasy journey.

CHAPTER

5

The Route From Issaquah

0   From Issaquah go south on Interstate 90 east toward Spokane

7.5   Take Highway 18 exit 25 toward Snoqualmie

11   Turn right onto Highway 202. Follow the signs toward the falls

11   After viewing the falls, get back onto 18 going south. Follow signs toward Maple Valley

25   At Maple Valley, turn south toward Enumclaw on 169

40   Get gas in Enumclaw

82   Turn right (west) on Stevens Canyon Road toward Rainier National Park Entrance. Follow signs toward Paradise Inn

103   Go west onto Paradise Road. This will become 706 toward Elbe

135   At Elbe, turn south onto Highway 7 toward Morton

152   At Morton, turn east toward Packwood/Randle

186   Arrive in Packwood

Get back on Highway 18 going south. After about 12 miles you take the exit toward Highway 169/**Maple Valley/Enumclaw.** This will take you out of the traffic and onto rural highways. On a weekend these rural highways could be choked with RVs and other traffic all eager to get away from it all. On weekdays you may encounter some truck traffic.

You might wonder about the pretty town of Enumclaw. It was named after nearby **Mt. Enumclaw,** which means "thundering mountain." Residents are proud of the horses raised in this area, as well as the low crime rate and good public schools. At the café where I last ate, the teenage waitress was proud of the mayonnaise on her sandwiches. To each his (or her) own.

Enumclaw is a great place to gas up since you will be entering National Forest land just out of town. It's fun to watch **Mt. Rainier** come closer and closer as you motor south through deep forests and sunny meadows.

Of all the Cascade volcanoes, Mt. Rainier appears the most massive. Perhaps that's because the ice age glaciers seemed to pass it by. About a million years ago Mt. Rainier was a low shield volcano covering 100 square miles. By about 75,000 years ago it reached its highest elevation. Since then constant glacial action has worn it down to a mere 14,411 feet—the highest point in the state of Washington. Most recent eruptions have been huge steam explosions during the 1960s and 1970s. Geologists expect it to erupt again some day. Don't turn your back to it.

CHAPTER
5

It would be easy to believe that there are no human footprints in the deep woods surrounding Mt. Rainier.

About 40 miles south of Enumclaw you will see the junction of Highway 410 and Highway 123. If you stay on Highway 410, you will end up in Yakima. You don't want to go there . . . yet. Keep going south on Highway 123. Eleven miles after the junction, turn right on Stevens Canyon Road to enter **Mt. Rainier National Park.** This is all well signed.

You will notice that the higher the altitude, the rougher the road becomes. It's difficult riding because the mountain floating in a blue sky, the milky glacial-fed streams, and alpine flower-choked meadows call for your attention. But the road has pot holes and cracks that demand your eyes. Lucky for us bikers, there are many turnouts. You get 19 miles of this road until you turn onto the Paradise Inn Drive. Two miles later you are in **Paradise.** Ah, the dream national park lodge.

Paradise Inn. Designed shortly after World War I, it pulls you in with rustic romance. Keep your camera ready as you stroll around the lodge and the meadows surrounding it. It's easy to see why nearly two million visitors come to enjoy the beauty and grandeur of Mt. Rainier National Park.

High points here include strolling amongst the wild flowers, gazing at the massive peak and glaciers of Mt. Rainier, and wandering around Paradise Inn. After enjoying the rustic exterior of Paradise Inn, I suggest hanging out in the lobby. The exposed log construction and paper lanterns give the room a homey feel.

While relaxing in the lobby, you can think about how Mt. Rainier National Park first became a park in 1899. Looking up at its summit, it's not hard to realize that it has over 35 square miles of surface covered with glaciers.

Looking across a canyon, the fir trees seem to reach up toward the mists.

Glacial runoff still flows through this glacial-cut riverbed.

Rustic strength comforts visitors to Paradise Lodge.

CHAPTER
5

Doesn't the sweetness of these turns make you want to visit Mt. Rainier?

You might think that leaving the Paradise Inn parking lot means your dream trip is over. Not so. You will head south on Paradise Inn Road toward **Elbe.** This twisty road seems to be in better condition than your way into the park. Take advantage of the pullouts for photos and a chance to see old growth timber, smell sweet mountain breezes, and listen to the still forest. Thirty-three miles after leaving Paradise, you will pull into Elbe. Named after a pretty town in Germany, you will leave this town and go south on Highway 7 toward **Morton.**

When I was growing up, my neighbors frequently talked about how good the pie was in Morton. Being a lover of pie, I could not believe how happy I was to pull into Morton the first time. Morton has many cafés and restaurants. Which one had the pie? I've never found the great pie of my dreams in Morton, but **Cody's Café** and the **Wheel Café** have good food. Locals swear by their Mexican restaurant, **Plaza Jaliso.** Still, every time I hear about the town of Morton, I think of pie.

Renting In Washington

The Evergreen State is the best motorcycle rental destination in the world. Largely due to a business called Mountain to Sound Motorcycle Adventures. This place rents just about any bike I've ever fantasized about riding: BMW, Honda, Yamaha, Triumph. I've rented with them before and had a blast on their bikes. They also rent gear, offer advice, and can put you into a motorcycle tour where all the details are handled for you. Their prices are hard to beat.

Mountain to Sound has a limited selection of Harleys. If Harleys ring your bell, Downtown Harley-Davidson and Destination Harley in Tacoma offer just about any Harley model for rent. These beautiful bikes are in top condition. Ask about free loan of helmet and rainsuit.

Ride West BMW is the agent for California Motorcycle Rental. They allow you the option to pick up a R1150R in Seattle and drop it off in Los Angeles.

Most of these rental businesses require that you be 25 or older, and that you hold a valid motorcycle endorsement on your driver's license. They vary on cost, insurance, and deposits. One-way rentals often involve a drop-off fee.

Call or check their web sites for other rental considerations.

Downtown Harley-Davidson
(206) 243-5000
www.downtownhd.com

Destination Harley
(253) 922-3700
www.destinationharley.com

Mountain To Sound Motorcycle Adventures
(425) 222-5598
www.mtsma.com

Banana slugs can be a hiking hazard in Mt. Rainier National Park. Watch your step.

From Morton it's only 34 miles to **Packwood.** Packwood itself is a great location for a biker to use as a hub for volcano exploring. It offers cheap, clean lodging, adequate restaurants, and puts a visitor within easy day trips of three great volcanoes and the spider web of terrific roads which always seem to cling to the sides of these geological monsters. Nearly any kind of road is within a few hours of Packwood.

My favorite place to eat and stay in Packwood is **Peter's Inn.** Many bikers eat breakfast at **Cruiser's Pizza.** With images of Rainier National Park, Paradise Inn, and the rural charm of The Evergreen State in your mind, you will need to decide where to go next. From Packwood you can connect to the Wild Side of Mt. St. Helens (Trip 19), or the Packwood to Cashmere Run (Trip 5), or make your own journey.

Packwood Food and Lodging

Cruisers Pizza
(360) 494-5400

Canoodle Inn
(360) 494-4522

Cowlitz River Lodge
(360) 494-4444

Crest Trail Lodge
(360) 494-4944

Hotel Packwood
(360) 494-5431

Inn of Packwood
(360) 494-5500

Mountain View Lodge
(360) 494-5555

Peters Inn
(360) 494-4000

Rest stops can refresh a bikers body and mind. Had I not stopped, I'd have missed these tiny flowers.

Trip 13   Crater Lake Tour

From California to Crater Lake to the Glass Mountain

Distance   *153 miles (yeah right). This is the mileage without really wandering around, taking the whole Rim Drive, or using the turnouts and so forth. I'd suggest two days and one night for wandering, short hikes, and gazing.*

Terrain   *About half the miles are on US 97, a busy two-lane highway. It won't be half the time, since 97 is pretty quick. Lots of twisting forest and mountain shoulder roads. Watch for deer and rocks near cliffs.*

Highlights   *Mountain air and forests, the eerie blue of Crater Lake, arid routes east of Crater Lake, and a mountain of glass*

The View of Wizard Island from near Crater Lake lodge is breathtaking.

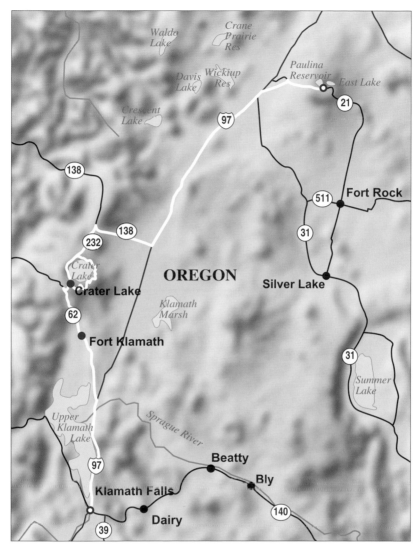

Sometimes, to give our life meaning, we need to take a chance. Edgar Lee Masters wrote that "to put meaning in one's life, may end in madness. But life without meaning is the torture of restlessness and vague desire. It is a boat longing for the sea and yet afraid." Maybe that's why we ride motorcycles. While many people cling to their televisions for meaning and life, we go out and experience it. We ride wild and free, the wind blasting into our faces—unless we dislike the feeling of smashed bugs on our cheeks and choose to wear a face shield. Still, we are free. Pretty much.

CHAPTER

5

The Route From Klamath Falls

0   Start going north on 97 (if you've been this way before, follow the west side of the lake on 140 through Rocky Point)

21   Veer left onto 62

51   Turn right onto Munson Valley Rd (follow signs to Crater Lake)

55   Follow signs to Rim Village or continue on Rim Drive

61   Turn left onto 232

70   Turn right onto 138 toward Diamond Lake Junction

85   Turn left onto 97

134   Turn right onto Paulina/East Lake Road (toward Newberry Crater National Monument)

153   Turn right into the Big Obsidian Flow Parking lot

Entering Crater Lake National park, bikers pay too.

The guard rail slid down the cliff leaving pavement right up to the edge of the lake. It was spooky parking this rental bike so close to the edge.

I think William Gladstone Steel was a man who traveled unafraid to his destiny. Except for the face shield part and the little obstacle that motor-cycles hadn't been invented when he was a youth, he might have been a biker. In 1870, Steel opened his sandwich and looked at the wrapper—a piece of old newspaper. There, at age 16, William Steel read about **Crater Lake** and a volcano of sorts rumbled in his mind. Two years later he would leave Kansas and move to Oregon, the goal of seeing remote Crater Lake bubbling in his head. Could it be real? Or are the tales of a seven-mile-diam-eter crater filled with pure blue water along the lines of man-eating trees, fire breathing dragons, and glass mountains?

Now if you're riding on your motorcycle as you read this, pull over before reading any farther, or you will surely crash. The lake that Will Steel dreamed about exists. And so does the glass mountain and the fire-breathing dragon. I'm going to tell you about a journey up from California to Crater Lake and beyond to a glass mountain. The fire-breathing dragon will be your motorcycle. If anyone knows where the man-eating tree is, let me know and I'll figure out a way to include it in this Journey.

CHAPTER
5

I'm beginning this story in **Klamath Falls,** a pretty, former frontier town near the California border. (Read Trip 24 to find out more about Klamath Falls on page 256). As you travel north on US 97, it's fun to watch all the birds on **Klamath Lake.** The mountains that frame this huge lake are the oldest in all of Oregon. They wear gentle shoulders like the well-worn mountains of the east coast of North America.

About 22 miles north of Klamath Falls, you turn onto Highway 62 toward Crater Lake. This well-signed road goes 14 miles until you get to Fort Klamath. I like to stop here because of the pretty valley/mountain views and the historical museum where you can see the original **Fort Klamath gatehouse** and view relics from the era of Modoc Indian Chief Captain Jack.

About 16 miles from Fort Klamath, you enter the park. Bikers pay $5 with or without passenger. I would head for the lodge ASAP to drink in the grand blueness of the lake. Follow the signs to **Rim Village.** See if you can look into the lake and not feel something move within your soul. The lake, larger than loneliness, lies silently sleeping in a vast crater, the deepest lake in all the USA. You can turn away and still feel the blueness.

Park your bike and stroll around the rim. Take a break from the blueness to explore **Crater Lake lodge,** eat lunch, or bathe in the immortality of the lake and its shores, chiseled by God.

If you book a year ahead of time, you are nearly certain to get a room in the grand old lodge. Otherwise you can stay in the 40-unit **Mazama Motor Inn** or the 198-site campground. The tiny towns surrounding the national park nearly all have motels. I've camped within the park before. When I did, I watched the light fade from the sky and lake. Linger until the stars begin to pop out. The show of stars nearly equals the lake.

Do you favor right turns or left turns? The 33-mile **Rim Drive** is a must. There are dozens of turnouts and interpretive signs. If you go counter-clockwise (left turns) around the lake, you can more quickly view the pinnacles—eroded pastel ash columns. Keep in mind that due to the over 44 feet of snow the park receives each winter, the Rim Drive opens for only a small window in the summer.

After you paid your $5, you rode right past the **William Steel Information Center.** You might be wondering if Steel ever got to see the object of his passion. Finally, in 1885, Will Steel hiked up the mountain with some friends. They stood at the rim of Crater Lake, startled by the vibrant blue waters. "All ingenuity of nature seems to have been exerted to the fullest capacity to build a grand awe-inspiring temple the likes of which the world has never seen before," wrote Steel of that moment.

Historic Crater Lake Lodge is a fine place to relax by the lake.

Passion about Crater Lake pulsed through Will's veins. He had to preserve it. From the moment of his first view of the lake to his death in 1934, Will Steel worked toward the protection and preservation of the lake. He poured his labor and personal fortune into the project. On May 22, 1902, **Crater Lake National Park** was established.

In 1909, Will Steel supplied the funding to begin construction of **Crater Lake Lodge.** Now you can stroll through this fine old lodge, have a meal in the dinning room, and sit out on a handmade rocking chair to gaze at the lake. Perhaps you will hear the wind sigh in the trees, or maybe that's the vague ghost of Steel yearning for you to feel his passion. The lake appears indifferent to all the fuss about it. But you won't feel that way. Once you see this place, you will understand what perfect blue is. I know of no other way to gain this understanding. The lake will move you.

CHAPTER

5

Turn your back to the lake on the north side and this view knocks your eyes out.

Dare you leave this lake? You must. But console yourself that you will be on a journey to view a glass mountain. Leave the lake, ignore its tug on your handlebars, and go north on 232 for about nine miles. Turn right onto 138. Locals tell me they go 90 mph on this 15-mile stretch of straight highway. But then, they have pick-ups with deer bars in front. You may desire to outrun the call of Crater Lake, but watch for deer and other forest animals.

Turn left on Highway 97. Separated by 70 miles of mountains and valleys, this beautiful road parallels Interstate 5. As a result, it gets heavy truck and tourist traffic. The gorgeous views are everywhere. Mountains, like a guilty conscience, linger silently on the horizon.

To get to the glass mountain, turn right on Paulina East Lake Road (toward **Newberry Crater National Monument**) about 10 miles north of **La Pine.** This is well signed. You will need to stop to pay a forest use fee of $5. Ask the ranger for directions to the **Big Obsidian Flow.** They'll tell you to stay on Paulina Lake Road for about eight miles until you see the sign for the Big Obsidian Flow parking lot.

Side Trip to Cascade Lakes Highway

Also called Century Drive because it used to be 100 miles long. Now it's about 80 miles long. Begin the ride just north of La Pine by following the signs to Wickiup Reservoir. From Wickiup, continue east until you get to Century Drive. Turn right (north) and enter dreamland. One of the most scenic and motorcycle-friendly roads in all Oregon. Spend the night in Bend or see if a room is available at Elk Lake Lodge: (541) 317-2994.

The Big Obsidian Flow is truly a mountain of glass. About the same time the Roman Empire was renamed the Byzantine Empire (550 AD), an eruption of glass occurred in this special place. Many of the rocks are obviously volcanic glass, but some of the stones look different. Instead of black opaque glass, they appear gray and dull. It turns out, all the rocks in the whole gigantic flow are chemically identical. Some rocks have more gas mixed in. Those rocks, although pure obsidian, appear like "normal" volcanic rocks.

You can hike the flow. The trail is only a mile and well worth the views of house-sized glass chucks. If you go in August, you may witness the strange phenomenon of the migrating frogs. Thousands of frogs, for reason

Hiking on the Big Obsidian Flow can be tricky: one slip and you'll need every Band-Aid in your kit.

CHAPTER

5

unknown to biologists, climb up the obsidian flow to disappear into the cracks. It's nearly impossible to avoid stepping on them. Perhaps a magic kingdom, guarded by glass blades sharper than steel, exists under the mountain.

I'm leaving you here on this glass mountain. What a place to be abandoned! Actually your choices from here are excellent. My first choice would be to take Century Drive past pristine Cascade Lakes and mountains. See the side trip for directions. You can connect to Trip 24 for a desert experience or to Trip 20 for my favorite way to cross the Cascade Range into the **Willamette Valley.** Maybe you want to strike out on your own to seek the man-eating tree or seek a vision, like William Gladstone Steel, that's been bubbling in your mind. Go forth to gain meaning in your life. Keep your face shield down.

Sparks Lake off Century Drive will delight photographers and nature lovers.

Elk Lake at sunset. These Cascade lakes are beautiful and unique.

Lodging

Crater Lake Lodge
(541) 830-8700

Mazama Village Motor Inn
(541) 830-8700

Mazama Campground
(Reservations not taken, usually not needed)

East Lake Resort
(541) 536-2230
(Stay right near the Big Obsidian Flow)

Best Western Newberry Station (La Pine)
(800) 210-8616

Timbercrest Inn (La Pine)
(541) 536-1737

CHAPTER
5

Trip 14 Wilderness Breakthrough

North Cascades Exploration

Distance *300 miles (all day—Break this into two rides if it's hot)*

Terrain *From suburban rush to rural scenes in just 10 miles. Slow, relaxed curves until you pass Marblemount, tight mountain twisties cut into solid granite, wide open desert, possibly windy roads at end. Be prepared for startling changes in temperature, rain, and heat. Watch for deer and rocks on the road. Be careful around rented RVs.*

Highlights *You must see the striking, remote, and beautiful North Cascades National Park. Bright, sharp granite mountains, silt-green rivers, mellow Methow Valley, and Old West eastern Washington towns. Great pie and fresh peaches.*

Fireweed grows near roadsides and open areas. In the background the Northern Cascades seem to jumble together for this photo.

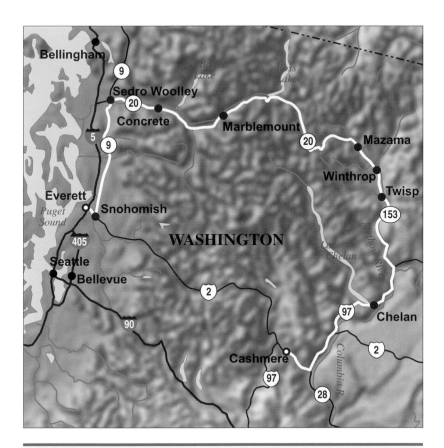

The Route From Everett

Here's the trip from Everett. From Seattle, go north on Interstate 5 to get to Everett.

0   Get on Highway 2 going east

2   Take the 204 East exit toward Lake Stevens

5   Turn north onto Highway 9

49   Turn east onto Highway 20

187   About two miles south of Twisp, take 153 going south

218   Turn right onto 97 ALT going south toward Chelan

227   When you get to Chelan, continue going south on 97 ALT

261   At Highway 2, turn west toward Cashmere/Leavenworth

276   Arrive in Cashmere

CHAPTER

5

The green Skagit River flows though some of the most rugged areas I've ever seen.

Some folks say this story began in 1814; Alexander Ross and four Indian guides set out to find a shortcut to the Pacific Ocean from the fur-rich valleys in Eastern Washington through the jumble of Cascade Mountains and forests. A fast way to get furs to the market would be worth a great deal. Using a storm that mowed down huge cedar trees "like grass before a scythe," the gods explained to the Indian guides that they were trespassing and should not continue their attempt to cross to the Pacific. Guideless, Ross was forced to turn back.

Four decades later, Henry Custer, working on a government commission, set out to find his way through the Northern Cascades using a western approach. Custer set out from the Pacific heading east into the Cascades. After scaling a tall peak, he saw wall upon wall of peaks and forests extending eastward as far as the eye could see. Although he explored over 1,000 miles of wilderness, he never made it through the Northern Cascades. Nearly 70 years of exploration finally revealed a way through these American Alps.

Men like Ross and Custer did open the mystic and massive Northern Cascades for the gold seekers and loggers to come later. Lucky for modern explorers on two wheels, this special place now has a beautiful highway passing all the way through it. Trip 15 will take you though canyons and forests, past grand glacier-clad peaks and into a beautiful, historic valley on the other side. There, you too will find gold, if the peaches are ripe when you pass through.

Start this journey just north of **Seattle** in **Everett.** Coming from Everett, Washington, Interstate 5 is the fastest way to get to this area and begin your own story of your journey through the Northern Cascades. If you have the time, I suggest you parallel the mighty I-5 by riding up Highway 9 just east of the interstate. So near the urban rush of Seattle, this is a pretty, rural highway. As you proceed north, it becomes more intensely rural, rolling and relaxing. Views of farms, tall hills just east of the road, and roadside fruit and corn stands punctuate this Highway 9 ride. Expect your speed to be in the 35 to 45 mph range.

Highway 20 starts off in a civilized way, running by pretty farms and cute towns like Concrete.

Sedro Woolley makes a fine stop for fuel and supplies before heading up Highway 20 into the wilderness. You might wonder about the name of this gateway town. In 1886, Mortimer Cook built a lumber mill on the **Skagit River** and named it Bug. His wife compelled him change it to the Spanish name for cedar: *cedro*. However Mortimer misspelled the word and the town became Sedro. Three years later a rival town and mill began operations just a mile away. Named Woolley after its founder, both towns abandoned an intense rivalry and merged when a depression hit the logging market.

If you don't pick up any logs or supplies in Sedro Woolley, you may have problems camping in **North Cascades National Park.** Most bikers do not stay overnight in the park. It's a drive-through experience for those of us who do not favor camping. Campers should bring all their food and gear with them, as services tend to be nonexistent near most campgrounds.

After loading up with supplies and leaving Sedro Woolley, follow the green Skagit River past peaceful fruit stands, small farms, and mixed forests. If you're hungry, I'd suggest you stop at the town of **Concrete.** At the **North Cascades Inn,** you can get excellent pie and a terrific salmon burger. Concrete gets its name from the limestone mines nearby. The region is still proud of its high quality cement made from local limestone. I like the town for its historical charm and pie.

Looking at the Northern Cascades from the east side, they look a bit tame at first.

After a break, it's time to blast through the canyon—keeping an eye out for rocks.

Once you reach the town of **Marblemount,** you truly feel you are at the last civilized place you'll see for a long time. A sign outside of town warns that there are no services for 69 miles. Originally this town developed to provide the gold and silver miners with supplies. Motels and somewhat seedy RV parks are scattered along the road near Marblemount. Once outside of Marblemount, the road shrugs off its lazy turns and gains energy, as the Skagit River appears even more milky green. Power lines and dams may intrude on your photos along this stretch. Energy-hungry Seattle sucks hydoelectrical power from the green waters of the Skagit.

The steep cliffs rising abruptly near the road may make you wonder how these rocks came to be here. Like so much of the Pacific Northwest, it began with volcanic lava. Unlike other volcanic rocks, the lava crystallized into granite, then yielded to deep uplifting forces. As a result of these amazingly unyielding rocks, the mountain peaks loom sharp and freshly cut, crystal cliffs push their chests toward your bike threateningly, and the V-shaped Skagit River canyons resist erosion. When you stop at pullouts, the North Cascades will pull a sigh from your lips. Such power and beauty!

CHAPTER

5

The Methow Valley welcomes travelers who've made it through the Northern Cascades.

The best glacier views tend to be at the end of hikes, since the road was only completed in 1972. Slides and rock falls keep road repair crews busy throughout the summer. Expect some construction delays when traveling the magnificent Highway 20 through North Cascades National Park.

Stop at the **Newhalem Visitor Center** for glacial viewing and tourist information, camping permits, and a chance to stretch your legs. As you motor through this 781 square mile national park, you'll discover some of my favorite parts on the eastern side, as you begin to follow the **Methow River.** If the skies were raining or spitting snow on the west side, it's likely the **Methow River Valley** will be dry—perhaps hot.

Leaving the wild part of North Cascades, **Mazama** stands first in line with services to collect travelers. Afterward, **Winthrop** beckons to tourists with a strong Old West theme. If you come through town on a weekend, it's tough to find a parking spot here. Once you push through the swinging doors of the saloon, no empty bar stools await you. Beautiful custom motorcycles proudly line the curbs. After the loneliness of the mountains, many people find Winthrop a refreshing contrast.

What I like best about the Methow Valley is the progression of mountains—from sharp granite blades, to more rounded saltshaker peaks, to the high, gentle rolling hills. I can imagine Alexander Ross and his guides starting here to find the way through the North Cascades, his trail broadened by gold seekers and ranchers who came afterward. As you break off Highway 20 after Twisp, you will spot more gentle hills and fruit stands. My advice is to avoid moderation when near these fruit stands. Many have picnic tables and allow you to eat as many peaches as you can buy. Peaches are the true gold of the Methow Valley.

Your goal for the night is **Cashmere,** but stop earlier if the heat, views, or peaches wear you out. One tourist stop I always enjoy is the "hip" town of **Chelan.** Latte anyone? Since the 1880s when miners and tourists flocked to this area, Chelan has been accommodating guests. Offering good food, lodging, and Lake Chelan—1,500 feet deep and 50 miles long—this place calls out for a visit. Only Lake Tahoe and Crater Lake are deeper American lakes.

The ranches on the east side of the park are served by mostly dirt roads.

CHAPTER

5

Getting Lower Rates On Accommodations

Chuck pulls up to the motel hot, tired, and near exhaustion. Standing in the motel lobby, a bag of clothing and toiletries hangs limply from his gritty hand. The hotel clerk knows that he will pay nearly any price for a room. Chuck asks for a discount and is turned down.

To negotiate a lower rate there are a few things a traveler needs to understand:

• Managers hate to have empty rooms. Renting a $200 room for $50 is better than an empty room.

• Managers are unlikely to lower a price if they are certain they can book all their rooms or if the person asking seems desperate.

• Managers need an excuse to lower prices. After all, they have their pride.

• Managers do not like to lower prices when other potential customers are within earshot or the person asking for the lower rate is objectionable. Be discrete and polite.

• Those people at the 800 number booking agencies have no authority to lower a price. You need to call the motel directly.

Phone Negotiation

It's often best to call ahead, perhaps even from the motel parking lot, sounding mildly interested or perhaps randomly curious about motel rates. When the rack rate is quoted, ask if they have any discounts available. Give the clerk an excuse to reduce their rate. Mention clubs, travel, and professional organizations. Explain why you are in the area. Be pleasant, perhaps even charming. When quoted a lower rate, ask if the clerk can find anything a bit lower. Ask for a business rate, a government rate, and a coupon rate (whether or not you have a coupon). Always ask for a discount if you are staying more than one day. Sometimes you can ask the motel to toss in a free breakfast if they have a restaurant. If the town is full of VACANCY signs, call another place if no discount is available.

Team Negotiation

Remember how Chuck entered the motel lobby? Now picture the way you would handle it. If you are traveling with a buddy or spouse, you enter the lobby looking as fresh, friendly, and relaxed as possible. Begin negotiations for a room by asking for the price and using the strategies mentioned in the phone negotiation. In addition, you can offer to pay cash. Minutes later your buddy can come in saying that he wants to stay at the next town. Friendly and polite, you ask the clerk for a reason to stay in this town—a lower rate. Your buddy reluctantly agrees to stay.

Sometimes you enter a busy town at high season, and you are lucky just to get a room at all. These strategies might save you a little bit of money if you pull into the motel in the afternoon. The manager wants to get everything booked and turn on the No Vacancy sign. But, like Chuck, you might just pay the rack rate.

Fireweed loves to grow on roadsides, clear cuts, and wherever a fire has opened up some sky.

CHAPTER

5

A last look back at the wonderland of the Northern Cascades; it's time for some flat land riding.

From Chelan, I'm going to send you down the west side of the **Columbia River** on Highway 97 ALT toward **Wenatchee.** Watch out for winds, particularly in the late afternoon. When you get to the junction of Highway 2 going west, turn left toward Cashmere. This simple town is where I like to spend the night and enjoy great food. See page 68 for information about where to eat and stay in Cashmere.

From here you can head south to connect to the Mt. Rainier journey (Trip 4), head east to connect with the Columbia Basin exploration (Trip 23) or turn your bars west to connect to any of the Washington/British Columbia trips. You can also make like the explorers Ross and Custer and find your own story, one that ends quite differently than theirs. Thousands of bikers love to take Highway 2 over Stevens Pass back to Everett (120 miles). Too bad our early explorers had so few choices.

Sedro Wooley

Chamber of Commerce
(360) 855-1841

Three Rivers Inn and Restaurant
(360) 855-2626
(Good beds, pool, blah food)

Newhalem

North Cascades Visitor Center
(206) 386-4495

Concrete

North Cascade Inn
(360) 853-8870
(Terrific pie!)

Winthrop

Farmhouse Inn
(509) 996-2191
(Probably the cheapest rooms in Winthrop)

Chelan

Visitor's Bureau
(509) 682-3503

Food

BC MacDonald's
104 E Woodin Avenue
(Great breakfasts and lunch)

La Brisa Restaurant
246 Highway 150 #11
PO Box 1764
(Mexican food)

CHAPTER
5

Trip 15 Olympic Peninsula Tour

Distance *400 miles without side trips (two days not counting side trips—three days is much more relaxing)*

Terrain *Few straight roads, many small towns on the southern part of the peninsula, possible heavy vacation traffic on summer weekends, rain likely no matter when you go. Deer and traffic are the main hazards. Speed limits mostly around 40 to 50 mph—a great touring speed.*

Highlights *Unique climate, Hoh Rain Forest, fishing villages, Olympic National Park, rugged coast, great seafood, more curves than a roller coaster, Hurricane Ridge*

I took this to show just how huge the Olympic National Park really is, but no photo can convey the enormity of this special park.

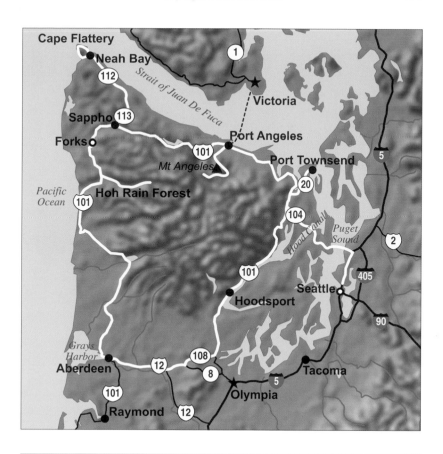

The Route From Seattle to Forks

This is without any side trips. Most people do not allow enough time to travel these legs. These are pretty slow roads.

0   Leave Seattle going north on Interstate 5 toward Vancouver, B.C.

14   Take the exit toward the Edmonds/Kingston ferry. Follow signs toward the ferry

18   Board ferry. When exiting ferry, turn left. Follow signs to 104 west

33   Turn right onto 101 north

144   Arrive in Forks

CHAPTER

5

This gravel road is the only way to get to Cape Flattery, but the view is worth the muddy bike.

Picture a map of the lower 48 states. Now name a place in the far southwest corner. San Diego, right? Name a place in the far southeast corner. Key West. You know what's coming next. Northeast? Eastport. Do you know what's on the northwest corner? Few people do.

This journey is about **Neah Bay** (NEE ah), the **Hoh Rain Forest, Olympic National Park,** and other treasures all remotely located on the **Olympic Peninsula** and connected by fantastic motorcycle roads. Just thinking about this unique place makes my throttle hand restless.

Just like it's hard to explain to a stranger why we like to travel on bikes, only after you visit a unique place like the Olympic Peninsula could you understand the thrill and power of this matchless region.

The power comes from ancient woods choked with gigantic trees. Growth and decay explode at time-lapse speed. Eight species of trees have their largest specimen on the Olympic Peninsula. These woods are so vibrant and full of life that plants grow on every possible surface.

Even tree trunks are covered with epiphytes. Epiphytes are plants that grow using other plants as a base. Unlike parasites, these plants give nutrients to their hosts. The Hoh Rain Forest throbs with gentle green that seems to emanate from the earth itself. There is no other place in North America with this climate.

The Olympic Mountains have no roads anywhere near their peaks, and even the paths seem shy about approaching these grand mountains. The highest peak, **Mount Olympus,** gets the equivalent of 220 inches of rain each year. This moisture feeds a complex system of massive glaciers which move as much as five inches a day. The jagged peaks of this range effectively remove so much moisture from the damp Pacific winds that the town of **Sequim,** only 40 miles from Mt. Olympus, gets only 12 annual inches of rain.

Marine fossils in the peaks of the Olympic Mountains tell geologists that these rocks were once sleeping under the sea. After rising up, an ice age brought 3,000-foot-high glaciers on a collision path with the Olympic giants. The rivers of ice broke upon the rocks of these great mountains and carved out **Hoods Canal** and **Puget Sound.** Lucky for bikers, the Hoods Canal area hoards some of the nicest biking roads in Washington.

Flowers and sharp, snowy peaks as far as the eye can see, this Hurricane Ridge stop is a must.

Besides the Hoods Canal area, bikers also love the rugged coasts, glacier carved valleys, lakeshores, and deep forests. I'm starting this journey from **Seattle,** but due to the ferry system, riders from all over the Pacific Northwest can begin this loop in a variety of places.

Leave Seattle and point your bike north on Interstate 5. Take Highway 104 west toward the **Edmonds/Kingston Ferry** (see sidebar on riding the ferry on page 52). Follow 104 west until you get to Highway 101.

You can take a two-hour side trip to **Port Townsend** to view its restored Victorians and stroll the busy shopping districts and waterfront.

Continuing on 101, follow the signs to **Port Angeles.** If you are stopping for food or accommodations, this town has good restaurants in the old town near the **City Pier.** You can picnic in the park and climb the observation tower to view the **Strait of Juan de Fuca.**

The best part of Port Angeles to bikers is the access to **Hurricane Ridge.** A biker can go from sea level to 5,300 feet in just 17 miles. Twisty! Keep your speed under control because of rocks, deer, rented RVs, and rangers. When you stop at the kiosk to buy your parking permit, ask about road and weather conditions at the top. Port Angeles can have warm sunshine, while the skies can be spitting rain/snow mix at the top. Bring hiking shoes because this wonderful road puts you at the highest paved-road point in the park. Taking a short hike can open views that will linger in your mind for a lifetime. Usually this area has limited visibility, so consider yourself lucky if you have sunshine.

Weather fluxes constantly at the top of Hurricane Ridge. You can have snow, rain, mist, sunshine and fog. (Photo by Sharon Hansen)

Oddly, the Olympic Peninsula has few beach outlets. Some have romantic names like Beach 2, Beach 3 and so forth. A trip to the beach is well worth it.

I know what you are going to want to do when you come down the mountain from Hurricane Ridge. You are going to want to hug the coast going west around the Olympic Peninsula. I have a better idea. Stay on 101 past **Lake Crescent** to **Sappho** and finally **Forks.** Here's why.

Highway 101 past Lake Crescent offers a biker wonderful turns and scenery. Since nine miles of the road runs along this beautiful, 1,000-foot-deep lake, many of the apexes are open for a biker to see. Once at the old **Lake Crescent Lodge,** a short lakeside hike will introduce you to the phenomena of temperate rain forests.

Motoring up the road from here, you can take a paved road up the **Sol Duc River** to the hot springs or hiking trail. Only $5 to soak your road-tired bones in the natural hot springs and more moss than you'll see anywhere besides this national park. Access is through the resort. At the end of the road, you can hike 3/4 of a mile in the woods to see the **Sol Duc Falls.** Bring your camera.

You'll travel this dark forest hallway on the way into the Hoh Rain forest.

Get back on 101 heading west so you can spend the night in **Forks.** I choose Forks because I'm a softie who does not enjoy motorcycle camping, especially in the rain. Forks is a large, friendly town possessing ample motel, restaurant, and other services. **The Coffee Shop** serves logger-sized breakfasts and the Asian restaurant, **South North Garden,** has good dinners. Look at the addresses at the end of this ride for places to stay.

Here are two must-see places on this wondrous Olympic Peninsula: Neah Bay, the end of the world, and the Hoh Rain Forest, the beginning of the world. First, The **Hoh Rain Forest.**

To get there, leave Forks going south on 101. Look for the well-signed Hoh Rain Forest turn about 12 miles south of Forks. Almost immediately upon turning off 101, you notice things are different in this wild place. A diaphanous green mist seems to linger just out of reach wherever you look. Millions of unnamed colors of green glow from every corner. Stop your bike at a pullout, close your eyes, and you can hear ancient, vibrant energy forcing itself on the woods. Perhaps emanating from the woods.

Pause at the visitor center to take the 3/4-mile **Hall of Mosses** tour and experience a walk within the vibrant halls of these woods. Perhaps all living things began in a pulsing place like this. You will come away feeling different about things. You must see the Hoh Rain Forest. Expect to put about 70 miles on your bike from Forks to Hoh and back again.

If the Hoh Rain Forest is number one, a close second is the trip to **Neah Bay.** Even though it's only about 50 miles from Forks to Neah Bay, allow yourself two and half hours for the ride. This is due to the wondrously twisty roads toward the end of the journey and the lower speed limits. On our last trip, we saw so many deer, the lower limits were appreciated. From Forks, go north on 101 to Sappho, then turn north on 113 toward Neah Bay.

Five hundred years ago a Mekah native tossed a wooden spoon into the forest. What's left of it now? Nothing, right? Present-day Mekahs were lucky enough to discover a buried village rich in well-preserved artifacts. As a result, you can learn about pre-contact Native life in their beautiful **Mekah Museum.** Filled with expertly presented exhibits, you must see the Mekah Museum. Try the **Mekah Café** for lunch or dinner; watch the harbor seals and birds as you eat.

This sweet road winds deeper and deeper into the heart of the rain forest.

CHAPTER

5

Mists cling to the tree tops as we prepare to venture out from our bed and breakfast in Forks.

You want to see **Cape Flattery.** To get there, you need to know the last mile is on a packed gravel road. I don't like taking my Valkyrie on unpaved roads, but the journey to the end of America is worth the trouble. A half-mile rain forest trail leads to views of **Tatoosh Island** and the crashing Pacific entrance to the **Strait of Juan de Fuca.** Bring binoculars and you will want to linger far too long at this magical spot watching the wild surf, whales (during migration season), the lighthouse, fishing boats, and other marine spectacles.

After Neah Bay and the Hoh Rain forest, you will think about completing your journey around the Olympic Peninsula. To do this, head south on 101 toward **Aberdeen.** From here you go east on Highway 12 for 20 miles, then take Highway 8 toward Olympia. This will take you past little towns: some perky and some drab. Once near Olympia take the short cut, Highway 108 north. This puts you on a wonderful motorcycle road along Hoods Canal: Highway 101.

The Route From Forks to Seattle (southern route)

0   Go south on 101

108   At Aberdeen, go east onto Highway 12

129   Veer left onto Highway 8 east toward Olympia

136   Turn left onto Highway 108 north

148   Turn left onto Highway 101 going north

236   Turn right onto 104 toward Kingston/Edmond Ferry. Board ferry to Edmond

237   Exit Ferry and take 104 east toward Seattle

242   Enter freeway going south toward Seattle

256   Arrive in Seattle

The tiny harbor at Sekiu can be photographed from a rest stop.

Hostelling

If you are traveling on a budget, you might want to consider staying in hostels. Hostelling is not only popular with the younger crowd, but it is now normal to see families and individuals as old as 80 using this low-cost lodging.

What are hostels? Years ago, hostels were budget accommodations featuring communal bathrooms and dormitory lodging. This type of lodging has been around for a thousand years, but became popular in modern times when a German school teacher named Richard Schirrmann began the hostel movement in 1907. He envisioned international meeting places where people could get to know each other and build "a bridge of peace from nation to nation."

Today's hostels are similar to budget hotel accommodations. Some hostels feature private rooms with bathrooms, smaller dorms, bars, restaurants, self-catering kitchens, laundry facilities, and Internet cafés. There are hostels in tepees, castles, lodges, mountain huts, and mansions. Our family stayed in a hostel outside Florence, Italy that was a renovated villa on gorgeous, manicured grounds. Hostels vary, so it is vital to use a hostel booking service or call the hostel to find out about their accommodations and facilities. Many are fully booked in the busy summer months, so reserving a room ahead is smart, especially in tourist locales.

You don't need a sleeping bag; in fact, many hostels won't let you use them as they may contain bugs. Many American hostels provide clean linens, towels, and blankets for your use. You need to bring soap and toiletries. Ask about towels when you call or book online, so you come prepared. Also ask about the neighborhood surroundings and available parking for your bike.

Does all this sound too good to be true? Here are some possible negatives as you consider hostelling: more noise, less privacy, and communal living. Some hostels advertise themselves as party hostels and others as family-friendly. Each hostel has its own atmosphere; if you are expecting meat and potatoes and get vegetarian-yoga-dreadlocks, you might be disappointed. Some are as messy as a teenager's bedroom. Others are painfully neat. Call and ask what to expect and read the online reviews.

The best way to book a hostel is online. Often these booking services feature customer reviews and list the amenities. Hostels.com has over 8,000 hostels listed and doesn't require a membership. Hostelworld.com has similar services and also lists other budget accommodations. They do offer membership cards for frequent hostellers or students. Hostelling International-USA is a membership group that offers discounts and free travel insurance to their members. Hostelz.com has great customer reviews and is free.

If you decide to give hostelling a try, be sure to allocate time to chat with the other guests. Even if you are hostelling in the U.S. or Canada, you will meet interesting people from all over the world. Isn't that what makes traveling so appealing?

Booking Sites

www.hostelz.com

www.hostels.com

www.hostelworld.com

www.hiayh.org

Do a Google search by entering the place you want to stay followed by the word hostel.

I like this road for its hills and turns, its canal views, clam chowder stands, and the way a biker can see through most of the turns. There are some casinos along this ride and I suggest you be aware of a higher-than-normal amount of impaired drivers near these places at any time of the night or day. Weekend traffic can also be annoying. Tourists love to drive this sinuous highway.

A good place to eat is **The Tides** on the left side of 101 just after you pass the town of **Hoodsport.** Great food, service, and painfully clean. **The Hoodsport Marina and Café** has great food, but it's closed on Tuesdays. Look for a blue building on the right.

To return to Seattle, you can retrace your route by turning east on 104 toward the Kingston ferry. While on the ferry you can think back on the wonders you've experienced: the mists of Hurricane Ridge, the sweet curves along Lake Crescent, the end-of-the-country views from Neah Bay, the green power of the Hoh Rain Forest, and a bowl of terrific clam chowder along Hoods Canal.

Lodging

Miller Tree Inn Bed and Breakfast
(800) 943-6563
www.millertreeinn.com

Forks Motel
(800) 544-3416
www.forksmotel.com

Dew Drop Inn
(888) 433-9376
www.dewdropinnmotel.com

Giant trees in Olympic National Park are common as chrome at a Harley store. This ancient cedar will grab your attention. Watch for signs near the Hoh turnoff.

This view of Tatoosh Island rewards hikers who are willing to go about a half mile from the end of the gravel road to Cape Flattery.

Bagby's Town Motel
(800) 742-2429
www.bagbystownmotel.com

Forks Chamber of Commerce
(800) 443-6757
www.forkswa.com

Food

Forks Coffee Shop
(360) 374-6769

North South Garden
(360) 374-9779
(Chinese)

Mekah Café
(360) 645-2789

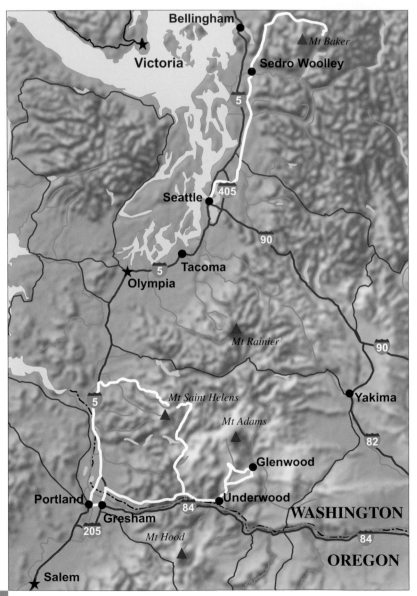

Only Volcanoes

Bikers beware: at this very moment, the great western Oceanic Plate grinds into North America's thin Continental Plate. Although this may only be about four centimeters each year, the result has a profound effect on motorcyclists. Ages ago this tectonic plate collision formed a fissure through which hard, smooth semi-liquid basalt flowed for eon after eon. This syrup-like basalt sealed fissures and filled valleys with oceans of basalt, but forces from the continuing collision of Oceanic and Continental plate found a way to punctuate the flat basalt plain: volcanoes. Good for us bikers who like wild, beautiful places with plenty of twisty roads.

Flowers and Mt. St. Helens dominate the McClelland rest stop. The rest of the ride is through deep forests and offers few glimpses of the peak.

The skeletons of hardy trees cooked by the hot blast of the 1980 eruption stubbornly remain standing.

The city of Portland has adopted **Mt. Hood** for its very own volcano since its white-shouldered presence dominates the skyline around the city. Lucky for Portlanders and visitors, this mountain has terrific biking roads. Much of these wander through impossibly deep forests of tall, thick Douglas fir trees. You can camp in remote areas, stay in rustic lodges, or relax in elegant, expensive inns while enjoying gourmet dinners. Mt. Hood offers just about everything.

Despite its massive size and proximity to Portland, **Mt. Adams** remains the invisible mountain. City folks know next to nothing about this secret place. Think of a friend who has a quiet sister. You can never quite remember her name, but you catch a glimpse of her now and then. She's pretty. You make a mental note to get to know her. This is Mt. Adams. It hasn't erupted for over 3,000 years. It's more massive than Mt. Rainier, but since Mt. Rainier sits on a high granite pedestal, Adams is the forgotten silver medalist.

Mt. Adams' small circle of friends includes huckleberry pickers, hikers and motorcyclists—all of whom can keep a secret. The Mt. Adams chapter reveals the best roads in the area.

Like Adams is to Portland, so is **Mt. Baker** to Seattle. It's so easy for a Seattleite to run down to Mt. Rainier, leaving Mt. Baker alone with its massive glaciers shining with all their might. The knockout views from this steep Cascade volcano look north to Canada's wonders, east to the endless peaks of the Northern Cascades, south to hills and valleys of western Washington and west toward the grand Puget Sound. The Mount Baker day trip requires a camera or binoculars to be tossed into the saddlebag.

My favorite of all the volcanoes in this book is **Mt. St. Helens.** This smoking giant offers the best motorcycling roads of them all. Earthquakes and volcanic activity can close some of the roads near the peak, but you can feel the heartbeat of an ancient forest as you travel the forest hallways surrounding the mountain. The eastern roads possess a wildness that can intimidate a newer rider, but the west side is perfect for someone just starting out or a fine day trip for a seasoned road warrior.

When you go over to the wild side of Mt. St. Helens, be prepared to rough it. Unlike the end of the Mt. Hood ride, no gourmet or even simple restaurants await a traveler. Fuel issues can be a concern if you ride a thirsty bike or dare to venture out without a full tank. Visitors are urged to read the chapters carefully for advice and suggestions to make these rides as pleasurable as possible.

If you have what it takes to explore these roads, you will feel the sort of satisfaction that is given only to bikers.

It would be a shame for the earth to do all the work of creating Pacific Northwest volcanoes, then to have them ignored by motorcyclists. I should caution you: once you get hooked on a volcano ride, all others may pale.

View the devastation caused by Mt. St. Helens looking toward Mt. Adams from the Cascade Peaks Viewpoint.

Trip 16   Huckleberry Loop: Portland to Mt. Adams

Distance   *190 miles (all day with rest stops and photographs)*

Terrain   *Some urban freeways getting out of Portland. Once you get onto Highway 14, traffic thins and the ride becomes relaxing and entertaining. Gentle rural roads for the rest of the trip. Watch for deer and other animals especially during mornings and evenings.*

Highlights   *Beautiful views of Mt. Adams, deep forest hallways and pleasant farms. Order something with huckleberries when in B Z Corner, Trout Lake, or Glenwood*

A visitor can get an idea of the massive nature of Mt. Adams from this shot. (Photo by Dave Gettling)

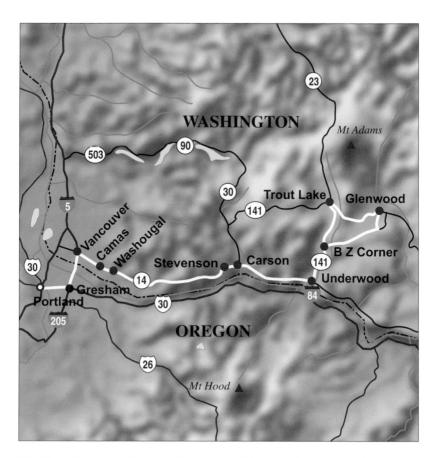

The first time you pick up a piece of petrified wood, you might just toss it away as any old rock. Touch a polished fragment of this stone, and it immediately makes you wonder about the value of this gem quality piece. For some reason, all the glorious mountains in the great Evergreen State get more attention than **Mt. Adams.** It could be because **Mt. Rainier** is higher, a national park, and adorned with tourist facilities. It could be that of all the high Cascade Mountains, Mt. Adams has the fewest roads on its steep flanks. It's the unpolished stone in the Cascade Mountain necklace.

A great number of visitors to the southeastern part of Washington do not go out of their way to see Mt. Adams, the oldest and second highest of Washington's volcanoes. Most of Mt. Rainier is about 75,000 years old, while Mt. Adams is about three times as old. Instead of the pretty older sister kept away from strangers, I think Mt. Adams deserves to be dressed in jewels and taken to a ball.

CHAPTER

6

The Route From Portland

0	Leave Portland
5	Take Interstate 84 east toward The Dalles
11	Take Interstate 205 north toward Vancouver
16	Take Highway 14 east toward Camas
61	Turn left onto 141 toward Trout Lake
80	Take the Trout Lake Hwy toward Glenwood
96	Take the Glenwood Hwy toward B Z Corner
115	Turn left (south) onto 141
123	Turn west onto 14
168	Turn south onto Interstate 205
173	Turn west onto Interstate 84
179	Take exit to Portland
184	Arrive in Portland

Begin this journey by heading east from **Portland** on I-84 toward **The Dalles.** Follow the signs to I-205 heading north to Vancouver. Once across the **Columbia River,** look for the exit to WA Highway 14 toward **Camas.** Just a few miles from the exit, you'll notice the traffic thinning and the road bending to track the smooth curves of the Columbia River. Just east of **Washougal,** look for the turnout called **Cape Horn.** I always stop here, even if I'm in a rush. The view is worth the time for a photo. Even though I own countless photos of this special place, I can't seem to stop myself from taking one each time.

When you get into **Stevenson,** you might want to stop at the **Columbia River Gorge Interpretive Center.** The exhibits feature information about Native American life, historical and economic influences of the Columbia River area. Admission is $6. It's also fun to stop at the posh **Skamania Lodge** and admire the gorge view from the lobby. Besides gas, in Stevenson, you can also get a decent breakfast in the **River's Edge Café** or run on to **Carson** for a true logger's breakfast at the **Wind River Inn** (located near the mill).

About 16 miles from Carson, follow the signs toward **Trout Lake.** Highway 141 winds away from the Columbia River following its tributary, the **White Salmon River.**

Doesn't it look like you could just drive right up to the base of the mountain? No paved roads come close to the base. (Photo by Dave Gettling)

Since this mountain usually hides behind the abundant stands of timber, it's a treat to see so much of it. (Photo by Dave Gettling)

If you happen to be in the area in mid- to late-August, you might notice hundreds of berry pickers. When you get to **B Z Corner,** you can ask where to pick **huckleberries,** although this is kind of like asking Fisherman Bob where his favorite fishing hole is. Do they want some strangers in their secret picking place?

Probably the best place to ask is at a ranger station. They also have maps. If you decide to go after huckleberries, do not pick more than three gallons. Exceed that, and you'll need a permit from the ranger station. The area around Trout Lake and B Z Corner is regarded as the best place in all the Pacific Northwest to pick these small, tart berries.

The road to Trout Lake offers some fine views of Mt. Adams, but many more views of pretty forest and farmland. Like a child, the big mountain seems to delight in hiding in the trees to pop out when you don't expect it. The road from Trout Lake to **Glenwood** has terrific views of the mountain, with aspen tree groves and sweet open meadows offering great foreground for your photos.

From Glenwood you can hook up to the Columbia River Basin exploration (Trip 1) or continue the loop back to Portland.

Once home, you can pop huckleberries and think about Mt. Adams, the kept sister of the high Cascade volcanoes. This gem of a trip might become a favorite.

BZ Corners

The Logs Family Restaurant
(509) 493-1402

Glenwood

Bird Creek Inn
(509) 364-3636

The Shade Tree Inn
(509) 364-3471
(800) 519-4715
www.discover-mt-adams.com

KJ's Bear Creek Café
(509) 395-2525

Serenity's
(800) 276-7993

Time Out Pizza
(509) 395-2767

Trout Lake Motel
(509) 395-2300
info@troutlakemotel.com

Trip 17 The Secret Roads of Mount Hood

Distance *110 miles one way (all day with early start and many stops)*

Terrain *Some suburban and rural roads, miles of little-traveled, narrow mountain roads, very twisty in places. Watch out for forest debris on roads and also animals, especially in early morning and evening. Some pot holes or gravel patches on forest roads. Roads may be still closed due to snow in early spring.*

Highlights *Rare and beautiful views of Mt. Hood, alpine lakes, and deep forests, wild flowers in mid to late summer, ancient Douglas fir trees*

The road to Timberline Lodge on Mt. Hood gives bikers wonderful views and turns.

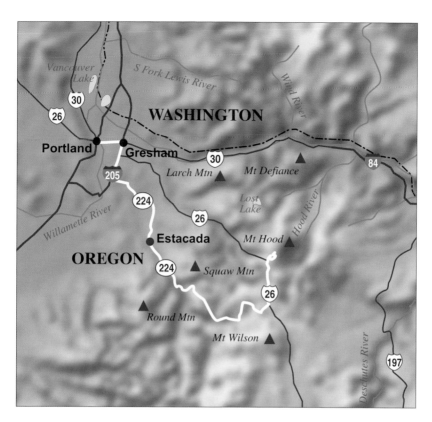

On October 29, 1792, a British naval officer reported, "A very distant high snowy mountain now appeared rising beautifully conspicuous in the midst of an extensive tract of low or moderately elevated land." This sighting let the secret of **Mt. Hood** out to all of Europe and America. Although this was the first white man's description of the mountain, it still appears the same and summons explorers. If you dare to ride in the vicinity of this great mountain, be prepared for the pull of the mountain on your handle bars. This chapter will give you the best way to yield to the force.

I'm going to suggest a route to explore this magnificent mountain that few natives have ever tried. Because the roads are so remote, few street maps even show the forest roads you'll take. Many of the available maps display these roads as unpaved. Other riders I've encountered on these roads say that they stumbled upon the route by accident. You can make a loop around the mountain on some of the most beautiful and secret roads in the Pacific Northwest. I suggest riders should make this a two-day ride in order to take little side trips and small hikes.

CHAPTER

6

The Route From Portland

0	Leave Portland going east on Interstate 84 toward The Dalles
5	Merge onto Interstate 205 (exit 6)
14	Take exit 12a toward Clackamas/Estacada (Highway 212/224)
16.5	Turn right onto 224/Clackamas Highway. Follow signs to Estacada
34	In Estacada, continue on 224
59	Turn left onto National Forest Road 4631 toward Ripplebrook
59.2	Turn left onto Road 57 toward Shellrock
67	Turn left onto Road 58 toward High Rocks
89	Turn left onto Road 42
95	Turn left onto Highway 26
106	Turn right onto Timberline Highway. Well signed
107	Arrive at Timberline Lodge

From **Portland,** head out toward **Estacada** off Interstate 205 and the beautiful, rugged **Clackamas River.** Be sure to gas up in Estacada, a timber town ridiculously named after the naked, stark Texas plains, Llanda Estacado. While in town you might want to take a peek at the **Rock House** (SW Lake and Beech), the oldest building in town, or the **Estacada Area Historical Museum** in the city hall.

As you leave Estacada, the road unrolls politely and properly along the sparkling pure Clackamas River. You will pass many shaded pull-outs where hopeful fishermen seek trout and silvery steelhead. Sharp-eyed visitors may find wild strawberries growing in sunny places during the summer. When you get to the boat launch at the **North Fork Reservoir,** you can stop for snacks and to chat with the fishermen. From the reservoir, State Highway 224 begins to stretch and twist like a waking giant. Trees shade the road and sometimes will hide the river from you. This part of the road is not secret, but well-known to bikers all over the state.

After a mile or so, the road becomes tighter and more energetic. It twists up steep hillsides away from the river in places. You pass wonderful campgrounds along this stretch. Indian Henry is one of our favorites. It's fun to fish for trout, hike the trails, and use their flush toilets.

CHAPTER
6

Few Oregonians have viewed Mt. Hood as seen from High Rocks.

Once you leave Timothy Lake, your first view of Mt. Hood from Highway 26 is a knockout.

Near **Indian Henry Campground,** you should watch for the signs to **Ripplebrook**—Road 57. Since most maps show this as unpaved, it has little traffic and much to offer the motorcyclist. Travel this fresh black ribbon winding into the forest during the morning, and warm smells of campfire smoke and cooking bacon will mix with the fragrance of the wild forest. Stop your bike at a turnout, and the sweet stillness of the backwoods will reveal hidden sounds of streams and breezes.

Ripplebrook offers no services for travelers other than advice. Many riders turn south on Primary Forest Route 56 at this place to visit **Bagby Hot Springs** (some gravel) and to continue to explore the Clackamas River canyons, but if you are eager to ride the Mt. Hood loop, stay on PFR 57 toward **Timothy Lake.**

About five miles after Ripplebrook Ranger Station, you will come to a fork in the road. Right leads to Timothy Lake and left winds steeply uphill to a rare and beautiful view of Mt. Hood at a place called High Rocks. Go left on Secondary Forest Road 4610 until the pavement ends. What a view! Tens of thousands of acres of deep forest making up the apron of the "beautifully conspicuous" mountain. At this point the pull of the mountain may be so great you will want to trade your bike for a hang glider just to get closer to the snowy volcano. Even in late summer the blooming wildflowers seem giddy with the pure mountain air and sunshine.

Backtrack to PFR 58 going east toward Timothy Lake. Soon you cross over the **Pacific Crest Trail** near some equestrian camp sites. You will likely come across mounds of horse manure on the road. Besides being slippery, it means that horses may be on the road. Be careful. This entire trip has only infrequent patches of gravel on the road, but occasionally you will find some forest debris, RVs, or a mad chipmunk frantically attempting to cross the one-lane road in front of you. Watch out for deer, especially in early morning and evening. I would suggest you not chug this road like a hot shot of tequila, but savor it slowly like a fine wine. Do not exceed your ability to stop on any blind curve. Tour, stop, listen, enjoy. The secret is out and you may be one of the first to know.

As you journey along PFR 58, you will be traveling through ancient old growth forests, cresting hills offering grand views of the **Mt. Hood Wilderness Area,** and sweet forest smells and sights.

A great rest stop is **Little Crater Lake Campground.** Well-maintained pit toilets and water are available, and the short hike to the tiny jewel of a lake in the woods is well worth the stop. The eerie water reminds me a bit of a Yellowstone pond. Cold (34°) blue artesian water filled an ancient volcanic blow hole and left crystal waters 45 feet deep. Some visitors claim a feeling of vertigo when peering down into the deep pure water.

From here you continue on PFR 58 toward **Abbot Pass** and **Timothy Lake.** Named for the timothy grass planted by shepherds, this lake was formed when a dam was constructed in the mid 1950s. Turn left at the junction of PFR 58 and PFR 42. You are headed toward U.S. Highway 26. Your goal is the romantic and beautiful **Timberline Lodge** and nearly the highest altitude you can take your bike in Oregon.

Turn left at Highway 26. Look for a sign indicating Timberline Lodge to your right. Timberline Lodge warrants a visit even if you do not decide to spend the night.

Built in 1937 by the WPA and dedicated by F.D.R, this beautiful lodge stands as a testament to the folk art of that period. Picture huge slabs of native stone and massive timbers, cozy seats close to a roaring fire while the night's chill descends, and a gourmet dinner in the **Cascade Dinning Room.**

Often we will eat a few miles down the road at **Don Guido's Ristorante** in the tiny mountain town of **Rhododendron.** Besides offering some of the best food on the mountain, the owner, Doug Kinne, greets each guest with his rich, deep voice that reminds me of Lorne Green from the show, *Bonanza.*

The fastest way down the mountain is to take Highway 26 back to Portland, but if you wanted to spend another day going around Mt. Hood, look at Trip 6—Hood River Fruit Loop.

CHAPTER

6

To head back to Portland, people in a hurry often take State Highway 26 to **Gresham,** follow the signs to Interstate 84, and buzz into Portland. It takes about 90 minutes from Mt. Hood. If taken during rush hours, give yourself more time.

It's been well over 200 years since Europeans first spotted Mt. Hood. Each day thousands of people notice Mt. Hood shining in their background. By taking this journey, you've experienced what few of them ever have: the secret roads of Mt. Hood.

Mt. Hood Food and Lodging

Timberline Lodge is a romantic and rustically elegant place to stay. Budget-minded travelers should stop by, get a cup of coffee from the bar, and enjoy the ambiance of a grand old lodge. The rooms were not designed as a luxury hotel, but more of a crash pad for outdoor lovers. Expect clean, comfortable rooms in a mature, artsy building. Great food. (503) 622-7979.

Stop at the Timberline lodge and stroll past all the folk art used to create and decorate this beautiful building.

The dramatic views of Mt. Hood from Highway 26 make it seem taller than its 11,239 feet.

Mt. Hood Inn is in the tiny village of Government Camp. It's relatively new in town and very modern, with microwave and small fridge in the room. (503) 272-3205.

My favorite place to eat dinner is Don Guido's Ristorante in the tiny town of Rhododendron. (503) 622-5141.

For breakfast, I like The Territory Restaurant & Lounge in Welches. (503) 622-1662.

A cheap place to eat and stay on the mountain is The Huckleberry Inn, (503) 272-3325, in Government Camp. They like to brag about their pie, but try one of their maple bars. Yum!

For small groups traveling, you can rent a little mountain cottage very cheaply in Welches at Cabin Creekside. (503) 622-4275.

Trip 18   Mt. St. Helens Loop: The Tame Side

Distance *242 miles from Portland, 300 miles from Seattle (all day with rest stops and photographs)*

Terrain *Some urban freeways getting out of Portland, possible wide swings in temperature from hot valley floor to chilly mountain breezes*

Highlights *Excellent views of the volcanic destruction and renewal of the Mt. St. Helens area, perfectly designed sweeping roads up the mountain*

On May 18, 1980, the bulging north flank of **Mt. St. Helens** collapsed. Magma and super-heated gas and ash, kept for centuries under unimaginable pressure, exploded outward at speeds over 800 mph. In five minutes, more than 230 square miles of forest were flattened. As a result, many of the roads had to be rebuilt. Lucky for motorcycle travelers.

Approaching Mt. St. Helens from the west gives a visitor a long view of the devastation.

Locals know this region to be two distinct trips. One is the tame and lazy western side of the mountain. Here you are likely to pass a Crown Victoria with gray-haired tourists out for a pleasant drive and a look at the stunning views of the volcano. You are also able to cruise some of the best engineered and most beautiful roads in all the state of Washington. On a typically clear day you should get excellent volcano photos and, depending on how much time you spend in the museums, a great understanding of Mt. St. Helens.

The Route From Portland

0.0   Take Interstate 5 north toward Seattle

65   Take the 504 exit (Exit 49) toward Castle Rock/Toutle

65.5 Turn right onto 504

121.5 Keep on 504 toward Coldwater Lake/Johnston Ridge

CHAPTER

6

Turn your back to the mountain to see where the blast went.

Beginning riders like this trip for the wide and forgiving roads. If you are on a rental, this is a great place to get used to your bike. Experienced riders enjoy the banked turns, views, and photo opportunities, as well as the interpretive museums. Often I bring visitors to this place just to make sure they have a great experience touring the Pacific Northwest.

The eastern side of Mt. St. Helens, Trip 18, is a dark and twisty ride where few mini-vans dare to travel.

A journey to the tame side involves some interstate travel through gentle valleys and billboard-framed small towns. Once off the interstate you can view such roadside attractions as an A-frame house partly buried in volcanic ash and a 30-foot-tall statue of **Big Foot.** This is the place to be to see the 1980 eruption interpreted through well-financed Federal museums. Keep in mind you will be ascending over 4,000 feet from base. It's typical to find temperature variations of 20 degrees from sea level. Bring gear to stay comfortable on this beautiful ride.

My favorite way to do this trip is to leave fairly early on a sunny Sunday morning. No traffic, no crowds, and a chance to eat a great breakfast in **Woodland, Washington.** If you must travel midweek, be aware that the **Portland** area rush hours can be hard on a biker, especially on hot days. I've found myself inching along, tire-to-bumper, at five mph for 10 miles. Portland has about 20 to 30 hot summer days each year, but many more slow freeway traffic days. Leaving Portland is better in the mornings since so many Washington residents commute to Portland each morning and return in the evenings. As you leave Portland in the morning, notice all the Washington plates going the opposite direction.

Once you are in Washington State and out of the city of **Vancouver, Washington,** you can start to enjoy the scenery. Interstate 5 parallels the **Columbia River** for 40 miles or so and you get occasional glimpses of the mighty river. (See the Highway 30 Portland side trip for a leisurely, and more scenic, way out of town).

The Coldwater Visitor Center has great views, bathrooms, and food.

Big Foot

Mt. St. Helens has an Ape Canyon and Ape Cave. It's easy to understand why. In 1924 a group of miners working near Mt. St. Helens shot and killed a large ape-like creature. That night apes surrounded the miners' cabin and tormented the occupants using ape howls, pounding, and stones. Somehow the miners survived the night and made their way back to civilization. Shortly afterward a posse composed of lawmen, loggers, and reporters returned to what is now Ape Canyon and searched in vain for the apes. Now Skammania County has a law against killing giant apes. If you see one of these creatures, do not harm it. You risk a $10,000 fine and a year in jail.

This part of the Pacific Northwest has pretty rolling hills, some grassy and some forested. Sadly, the little towns are nearly all framed in ugly billboards that clamor for your attention. Some visitors like to swing off the road and visit the poker parlors of hilly **La Center.** I always like to take a break in Woodland. Many riders will make Woodland a stop if they are planning a trip up to the eastern side of Mt. St. Helens. The best breakfast in town is at the **Oak Tree Restaurant.** To find this place, take the Woodland exit and turn right like you are taking 503 north. You will see it on the left about 300 yards off the freeway.

Continuing north on Interstate 5, make sure you take the 504 exit (exit 46) toward **Silver Lake.** There's a fine **Mt. St. Helens museum** near Silver Lake offering video and still images of the eruption that sent billions of pounds of ash all over the globe. I've noticed that most motorcyclists are so eager to see the mountain, they slip right past it. Highway 504, also called the Spirit Lake Memorial Highway, offers 52 miles of world-class motoring, but part of the fun is to stop along the way. On my way to the road's end, I always stop at three places: the Hoffstadt Bluffs Visitor Center, the Forest Learning Center, and the Coldwater Ridge Visitor Center.

Hoffstadt Bluffs Visitor Center offers you a chance to see the devastation and recovery in a way unique to most mountain views. With the trees gone, the naked slopes reveal their streams, boulders, and hills in a way you can't see in other places. The restrooms are clean, too.

Take out your binoculars when you stop at the **Forest Learning Center,** because you will likely see the resident herd of Roosevelt's elk, one of only four subspecies of elk to survive exposure to modern civilization.

At the **Coldwater Ridge Visitor Center** you start to find yourself at some serious altitude—3,091 feet. Here you can learn how the mountain's slopes, practically sterilized of all living things in 1980, are recovering. They have a video wall presentation that gives a visitor a good overview of the whole cataclysmic eruption. You can also stop at their café for a sandwich, soup, salad, or drink or check out the gift shop, book store, and a staffed information desk. I usually pick up my parking pass here.

The apex of this trip is the **Johnston Ridge Observatory** (elevation 4,255 feet). Here you can visualize the blast zone and get the best view of the lava dome and pumice plains, as well as the most close-up view of the mountain. Camera buffs, this is it! There are also interpretive exhibits that focus on the geological forces behind the eruptions. I like to toss some hiking boots in my bags so I can take one of the many hikes and stretch my legs before the trip back. No food available here, but clean restrooms.

You can check out the view in real time by going to this web cam address: www.fs.fed.us/gpnf/mshnvm/volcanocam/. Be careful. Viewing this pretty place may make you want to drop what you are doing, in a most uncivilized way, and blast off toward Mt. St. Helens.

Silver Lake Motel and Resort
(360) 274-6141
Rustic (outhouses outside) cabins can be rented at the county park. They have a nice lodge with motel rooms, also.

Silver Lake Park Whatcom County Parks & Recreation
(360) 599-2776
parks@co.whatcom.wa.us

Streeters' Resort
(360) 274-6112

Volcano View Resort
(360) 274-4457

Trip 19   Wild Ride: Carson to Windy Ridge

Distance *250 miles (all day with rest stops and photographs)*

Terrain *Some urban freeways getting out of Portland, possible wide swings in temperature from hot valley floor to chilly mountain breezes. Dress for it. Possible high-speed winds on top. Very likely to encounter rocks on the road, forest animals, uneven or ridged pavement, and packs of adolescent, racing sport-bikers on weekends. Remote roads many miles from services. Bring water.*

Highlights *Most curves per mile of any trip in the Pacific Northwest, eerie dead forests—standing and floating—a look into the throat of an active volcano, deep forest views, smells, and feelings, excellent views of the volcanic destruction and renewal of the Mt. St. Helens area*

This close to the peak, all the trees were blasted away. This allows a biker to see more of the roads.

CHAPTER
6

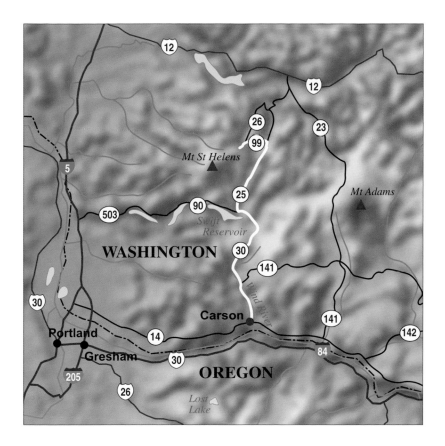

The Route From Carson

This whole trip is well signed. At each intersection, look for the roads to Mt. St. Helens/Windy Ridge.

0   Go north on Wind River Road (Highway 30). Part of this will become Highway 90.

31   Continue on Highway 90 toward Mt. St. Helens/Windy Ridge

36   Turn north onto Highway 25

62   Turn left onto 99

80   Arrive at Windy Ridge. Check the table below for your next destination.

CHAPTER

6

With your back to the mountain, this is the view of the pretty road you will travel home.

This ride is all about deep forests, wind-lonely naked hills, and the roads that twist through them. Going north from **Carson** on Forest Road 90 (also called Wind River Road), you find yourself in the **Columbia River Scenic Area.** Forest cutting and building is severely restricted in this area. Good for tourists. The Wind River Highway follows the writhing **Wind River** up the shoulders of the **Gifford Pinchot National Forest.** Far below the highway, fishermen are pulling salmon from the cold, clean, timeless waters of Wind River.

I'm starting this journey from **Carson, Washington.** Why Carson? Coming from **Portland,** it's the last place to get gas for 80 miles. It also is a mill town. Mill towns mean great breakfasts in the simple restaurants and proximity to the rich forests that supply the timber.

I remember a November fishing trip when my buddy Eric and I scrambled over frost-slippery rocks to get to the best fishing holes. We hiked past natural hot spring pools warming a few naked fishermen. We tried not to drop our fishing poles: all this for 60 pounds of fresh, wild salmon. When you cross over the **Conrad Lundy Jr. Bridge,** which is in the National Register of Historic places, you can think about the salmon and fishermen far below in the wild canyon.

Shortly after you cross this bridge you get a taste of things to come: twisty, forest-shrouded roads. As you enter the **Trapper Creek Wilderness** area, you notice the trees: Douglas fir, western hemlock, western red cedar, white pine, and true firs. Only locals are not amazed by the size and density of these trees whose pitchy breath scents the air. The dark, sweet forest smells and the many unnamed colors of green will stay with you almost the entire journey.

I'd like to say that these roads are as virgin as the woods, but somehow motorcyclists from all over the Pacific Northwest have found out about this special place. As a result, if you dare to come up these roads on a summer weekend, you will find dozens, maybe hundreds of mostly sport bikers. Sadly, a mixture of the youthful misconception of invulnerability, high performance bikes, testosterone, and competition have made roving packs of racing bikes a menace to tourists as well as themselves.

The roads are truly remarkable for the thousands of turns, many with perfectly revealed apexes, pavement, and banking. My heart starts to beat fast just thinking about them right now. In addition to the perfect conditions, a traveler can also find many difficult turns and plenty of grim law enforcement officers who are sick and tired of scraping smashed up bikes off the road, rocks, and trees.

Look at the white area on the right side of Spirit Lake; those are corpses of thousands of trees floating silently on the lake.

Even when the mountain is peaceful and still, it still possesses a certain malevolence.

Reg Pridmore, three time AMA Superbike Champion, writes that each blind turn should be taken as if there is a dead horse in the road just out of sight. Indeed, I can guarantee that you will find rocks, gravel, and forest debris on the road. I've never run across a dead horse, but the woods are full of deer and other forest animals that are particularly active at dawn and dusk. You will encounter dozens of places where the road is rough due to sunken grades, tire swallowing cracks, patches, or potholes.

You might wonder: If this place is so dangerous, why go? I go because it is so beautiful, so remote and wild, and it's the curviest journey in the whole Pacific Northwest. I go because natural power beats from the chest of ancient woods and unspoiled canyons. I go for the views of volcanic destruction, which haunt my mind right now. There is nothing to compare to motoring past a dead forest of trees pounded by an 800 mph volcanic wind of super heated gases and grit. To stand looking down at **Spirit Lake,** silent save for the breezes that might be the sighs of primeval trees giving up their spirits to float in sleep, is a unique experience. No place on earth is like **Windy Ridge.** Go.

About 20 miles from Carson, you will come across the McClellan Viewpoint. Besides some clean pit toilets, bright wild flowers, and picnic tables, you will find splendid and revealing views of **Mt. St. Helens** from the southeast vantage point.

In 1853, a young West Point-trained engineer named George McClellan tramped through these woods looking for a railroad route and, despite his reputation as a brilliant engineer, declared the forest "utterly worthless for any purpose . . ." McClellan would later lead the Union army during the civil war and show that a good engineer does not a great general make.

Some genius engineer made the road from the McClellan Viewpoint onward. Not only does a traveler have unexpected grand glimpses of the Cascade Mountains and their many valleys, peaks, and waters, the trees show an energy, size, and age that uplift a motorcyclist's outlook. People in cars miss so much! The roads are well signed and you needn't worry about getting lost. Keep toward the signs that indicate Windy Ridge. You will pass the **Eagle Cliff Store** a few miles after the McClellan Viewpoint. Here you can get refreshments and use the public bathroom. On weekends, the parking lot is often full of bikes.

At the next junction, turn right toward Windy Ridge/**Randle.** This is Forest Road 25, a bit more traveled—but just as twisty—as FR 90. From this junction, you have 15 forested miles until the well-marked FR 99 turnoff to Windy Ridge.

A motorcyclist can picture all the curves in this road as a chance to practice turning techniques. If you take a motorcycle class or read a book like Reg Pridmore's *Smooth Riding the Pridmore Way* before setting out, by the time you return, your daily turning skills should be greatly improved. For example, in *Smooth Riding,* Pridmore discusses using tight apexes as a safer technique than the late apex approach touted by many other safety gurus. After reading all the theory, spending six hours on all sorts of curves can really pay a dividend in skills. Dare to be a better biker.

Getting close to the mountain, this biker keeps his attention on the road. (Photo by Mike Means)

I mention this here because FR 99 has quite an abrupt rise in altitude, besides being more twisty than a brick of ramen noodles. Watch for trees that have been topped by the May 18, 1980, blast. They tend to be the highest of the old growth. **Old growth:** these huge trees possess a strangely timeless and abiding grace that can only come from living for hundreds of years. Perhaps they solemnly watched George McClellan resolutely tramp through. Today they stand in their forest—quiet save for the thin cry of a hawk soaring high overhead. Stop your bike to listen.

When you pass the boundary to **Mt. St. Helens National Volcanic Monument,** you'll notice the highway changes to gray and the forest takes on an even more ancient and vibrant feel. You are very close to the epicenter of this wild journey: **Windy Ridge.** Stop your bike to listen to the woods.

When the mountain erupted, thousands of tons of ash were blasted away from the volcano. Photos taken shortly after the event appear to be taken in black and white—everything is gray. Like scars across the breast and shoulders of a perfect statue, the roads writhe on the gray mountains showing nearly every curve. You may want to goose the throttle and get some serious lean angles. Remember the falling rocks. Monitor stations record humanly imperceptible earthquakes daily. Rocks or gravel will be on the road.

From the parking lot of Windy Ridge, you can attend a ranger talk and take the short hike to the lookout. You can watch the wildflowers innocently tremble in the wind or stare into the exquisite crater of Mt. St. Helens. Look closely at the lava dome. Will it erupt while you are standing there? Before 1980, it last violently erupted in 1857. Geologists expect it to explode again. Don't stare too hard; you might start it going.

Retracing your way back, you can stop for a quick meal or souvenirs at **Cascade Peaks Viewpoint**—just a few miles from Windy Ridge. To go home, you will need to retrace your route down FR 25. If you are going to Randle (nearest gas, food, and lodging and best route to **Seattle**) or linking up with the journey from Packwood to Cashmere (Trip 5), watch for the sign for FR 26 about eight miles from the Windy Ridge parking lot.

If you are headed to Portland, the fastest way there is to backtrack for some of the way. Stay on FR 90 toward **Cougar** (gas, food, lodging)—60 miles in all. This route takes you on new, sinuous roads along **Swift Reservoir, Yale Lake,** and **Lake Merwin.** Signs pointing to I-5 are easy to find. See table for distances.

This journey is more than a simple, large breakfast, wild canyons, still forests, and grand volcano ride. It's more than just a chance to practice turning techniques amongst ancient trees. This journey is a chance to touch an awesome power and terrible beauty. People in their cars would never understand this ride. They'd see some pretty views and gripe about the windy road. We know better. We make our sign to the wild void and journey on.

Distance From Windy Ridge To:	
Cougar	60 miles
Randle	36 miles
Carson	80 miles
Portland	112 miles (via Cougar and Interstate 5)
Seattle	150 miles (via Randle and Interstate 5)

Food and Lodging

Wind River Inn
22 Hughes Road
Carson, WA 98610

Carson Mineral Hot Springs Resort
372 St. Martin's Springs Road
PO Box 1169
Carson, WA 98610

CHAPTER
6

Trip 20   From Seattle to Mt. Baker

Distance   *250 miles (one day)*

Terrain   *Slow, rural highways along Highway 9, faster roads as you approach Kendall along the north fork of the Nooksak River. Poor pavement near summit. Check road conditions before leaving—Mt. Baker likes to brag about its long snow season. Watch for deer.*

Highlights   *Rural sights along Highway 9, climate change as you rise to over 5,000 feet along the shoulder of Mt. Baker, view of this wild country near the Canadian border*

The last volcano. **Mt. Baker** ends the chain. Past this steaming mountain, no more Cascade Mountains exist. Travelers could easily ignore this jewel of northern Washington. Mt. Baker, called Koma Kulshan (the steep white mountain), seems to have other ideas about this. In 1975 this forgotten child of the great Cascades announced it was worth watching by blowing off impressive amounts of steam and ash. Visible for miles, this glacier-gouged

Once you get to the top of the Mt. Baker road, this view rewards you.

mountain showed it was not asleep. After a few weeks the eruption settled down to a modest, but consistent, steam cloud issuing from a crater just south of the peak. Even today, viewers may see a steam cloud hovering near the white shoulders of Mt. Baker, especially on a clear, cold day.

The Route From Seattle

0   Leave Seattle going north on Interstate 5 toward Vancouver, B.C.

5   At exit 171, turn right toward 522 Bothell

16   Leave 522 by turning right onto Highway 9 north toward Snohomish

88   Turn right on 542 (Mt. Baker Hwy.)

124   Stay on 542 toward Maple Falls/Glacier. Continue on to road's end.

CHAPTER

6

As you motor along Highway 9, watch for Mt. Baker peeking out from behind the foothills.

Most travelers will journey to Mt. Baker by beginning in the **Seattle** area. Think of this mountain as 31 miles due east of **Bellingham.** If you are pushed for time, you can blast up Interstate 5 to Bellingham. Take the 542 E/ Sunset Drive exit (exit number 255) toward Mt. Baker, and follow the signs. You can be at the summit of Mt. Baker in less than 4 hours.

I suggest you pack a picnic and take the hill-hugging roads that parallel Interstate 5. Washington Highway 9 is an example of these parallel roads—rarely any more than 10 miles away from I-5, it seems a whole world away. Quiet, curving rural highways wind past hay farms. Ah, the smell of fresh cut hay. Past dairy farms. Ah, the aroma of fresh dairy farms. Oh well. It's still my favorite way to travel to Mt. Baker. If you can make your trip during the week, you will wind through small towns and hilly farms at 35 to 50 mph, your face shield up the whole time to enjoy the country air.

Continuing up Highway 9, you pass through small towns that appear dependent on the tourist traffic from Seattle. During late summer the fruit and vegetable stands pop up like dandelions in my lawn. Riding through here, I've always wanted to buy some of the fresh corn being sold out of pickup truck beds, but how to cook it when on the road?

Once you pass **Sedro Woolley** (see story on this town's name on page 172), the hills just to the east start to crowd in on you. As they get closer, the farms, woods, and hill-summits all become a bit exaggerated, as if the greens are greener, the farms more quaint, the hills tall enough to pretend to be mountains. Best of all, the roads become more up-and-down-and-twisty. I love this part of the trip.

At Kendall, turn right on 542 toward Mt. Baker for the 35 mile run up to **Artists Point** and the **Heather Meadows Visitor Center** (no food, picnic ok). You notice the road dives into a mixed forest. As you travel up this road, you'll see the bed and breakfast signs seem to multiply like rabbits. I've never stayed in one of these, but this road, air, and views make a person feel peaceful.

After the townlet of **Glacier,** habitation abruptly eases off and the road becomes rougher. Expect cracks and potholes to become more pronounced as the road gains altitude. Some of this might be due to the 500 inches of winter snow that Mt. Baker collects each year. Since you need to go slow due to road conditions, you might as well take advantage of pull-outs for photos and deep breaths of clean air.

Grandpa and this little helper were selling sweet corn from the back of a truck. Too bad I didn't bring a pot.

CHAPTER
6

Once at the summit, you will find yourself taking the loop around a small lake. When you look at the peak reflected in these waters, you can think about how this mountain was named after a young lieutenant, Joseph Baker, who spotted this white giant when on watch for British explorer George Vancouver in 1792.

Called **Artist Point,** this end-of-the-road spot is 5,140 feet high. It gives you views of hundreds of other mountains, valleys, and forests in Northern Washington. It is also a Northwest Forest Pass Site. Make sure you buy the pass to support this area and avoid a ticket.

At 10,778 feet, this last jewel in the Cascade chain of mountains is the most heavily glaciered peak in the whole group. If you combined the glaciers of all Cascade Mountains (except Mt. Rainier), their glaciers would be less than Mt. Baker. At a mere 30,000 years old, this ice-clad peak is considered to be young by volcano standards and the youngest of all the Cascade volcanoes. Geologists believe an old, 400,000-year-old peak lies under the present cone.

On the way down you may notice the tight switchbacks as the road strains to lose 3,200 feet in only 10 miles.

Down from the mountain, my favorite place to stay is the little Dutch themed town called **Lynden.** The newest and most posh place is the **Homestead Farms Golf Resort.** The cheapest place is the **Windmill Inn** just

Woods, rock, roads, and crystal air: what more do you want?

Highway 9 offers pleasant, curving roads which seem to cuddle up to the farmlands and wild places.

south of town. When you stroll the streets, you feel the pride and prosperity that embraces this town. If you decide to press on to the north to connect with one of the British Columbia rides, you will see hundreds of mountains, but not one of them will be a Cascade—you've conquered the last one.

Lynden Food and Lodging

Dutch Mothers
405 Front St.

Some Place Else
1806 18th St.
(360) 354-4299

Dinner The Loft
444 Front Street
(360) 318-1903

Windmill Inn
8022 Guide Meridian Rd.
(360) 354-3424

CHAPTER
6

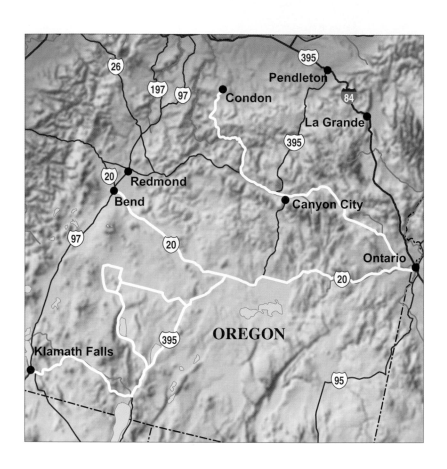

Desert Explorations

There's a reason the eastern parts of Oregon and Washington are so sparsely populated and so little traveled. It's not due to a lack of beauty or perfect roads. When you ride these roads on a bike, it's hard to imagine why these areas are not packed with two-wheeled travelers.

Most people on these roads are passing through. They settle back in their cars and trucks and don't even notice what we bikers treasure: a fragile beauty that refuses to be disturbed by the absurd actions of humans.

Some of these roads appear to have been precision-machined by a laser beam: so straight and true are they. Other roads struggle through steep, rocky canyons like a headless snake writhing to find its sight. When you ride these at dawn or dusk, they impart a sweet magic and joy to a rider. The trip from Bend to Ontario will always reside in a special place in my mind for the dawn revelations the desert gave to me the first time I rode it.

Gigantic hay bales form a shady spot that allows a rider to stretch and snap a photo of the high, brown mountains.

Near Lake of the Woods, snow and ice remain through Spring. Two weeks after this shot, the lake was summoning fishermen. (Photo by Sharon Hansen)

If you try the Christmas Valley Triangle ride, you will get to see the desert ride that converted me to be a dedicated desert rider. Startling and powerful images are burned into my mind: the highest fault scarp in North America, an alkali lake full of brine shrimp, a dune swept desert, towering brown basalt crags high above the shallow lake-bed valley floor.

Many Californians, on their way to Sturgis or some other destination, are unaware of the treasures between Klamath Falls and Burns. These include the town attacked by Japan during World War II, some of the oldest mountains in whole Pacific Northwest, an erupting geyser near Lakeview, old west towns that are still old west towns, forests, deserts, cliffs, and beautiful roads that will call you back to explore all the side roads. Don't stare at a map of this area too long; you will plan too many side trips. This is beautiful country.

In these chapters you will find some hard-earned advice on hot weather riding. Unlike some parts of the country, the Pacific Northwest is rarely humid. This means that a rider in hot country is better off wearing full armored gear, full face helmet, boots and gloves with a wet neck cloth and wet sweat shirt under that vented-armored jacket. The miracle of evaporation will keep this rider comfortable, as long as he's moving.

I'll never forget a ride in triple digit temperatures where we left a rest stop with all our gear over our wet things. A few miles into the ride we came across a bridge repair where we had to wait 20 minutes, pull forward a couple of car lengths, then wait more. This is one of the worst possible situations for a biker since there's no evaporation and it's impossible to suit down since you need to keep moving. This can also happen in stop-and-go traffic when passing through a city.

When you think of the great Pacific Northwest, don't images of forests and coastal landscapes come to mind? In this section of *Motorcycle Journeys Through the Pacific Northwest,* you will find out about the wildest and most remote parts of Oregon and Washington far from the lush coast and deep forests of these great states. These wild parts offer evidence of an even wilder time: an era of saber-tooth cats and giant ground sloths roaming this unique place. A place with desert colors and formations that seem placed there just for the biker. Car travelers don't seem to notice them.

Since the best biking roads in the whole Pacific Northwest lie near **Condon,** a biker who rides just for the joy of riding should plan a visit to this area.

Economic and environmental forces serve as an impediment to development of these special places. You may not be able to make a living in this part of the great Pacific Northwest, but you can accept its rough comforts as a two-wheeled traveler. If you explore these routes, you will be the trekker who has the sense of adventure and appreciation of raw beauty. Others may avoid these wild areas, not you.

Trip 21 From Bend to Ontario

Distance *271 miles (six hours with rest stops, meals, and photos)*

Terrain *Some laser beam straight roads, canyon sweepers, country roads, and small town slow-downs. Hazards include a tendency to go too fast, desert animals (especially near dawn and dusk), possible rocks and gravel near the base of cliffs, and weather.*

Highlights *High desert roads, desert beauty, Old West history, dramatic geological formations, Malheur River Canyon*

Locusts. The first one hurt. I remember a numbness in my knee. The next two came rapidly after the first, then suddenly I felt like a target in a paintball game. Traveling at desert speed, my bike, covered in oozing crushed bugs, I blasted through the locust cloud into a stillness that only a desert at dawn possesses.

Only about 80 miles to Ontario, the desert highway seems too straight to be real.

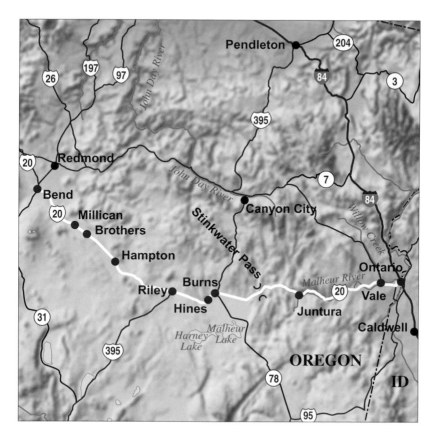

Some view a desert ride as an obstacle or a journey that must be endured. To others the desert can show its unashamed nakedness to riders willing to notice it. Dawn is the best time to notice. Travelers in cars could never understand the joy and beauty of watching the cold pink and purple shadows, the rocks, bluffs, and secret gulches that the early light reveals. Car travelers cannot smell the sweetness of the morning and cherish its freshness. Later on, when the sun is a hammer against the unforgiving anvil of the hot desert, the cool dawn sweetness seems even more precious.

The Route from Bend

0 Leave Bend with a full gas tank heading out on Highway 20 toward Burns

262 Arrive in Ontario. Follow signs to Interstate 84 to get to motels and restaurants

CHAPTER

7

Sometimes the green of irrigated land rests the eyes of a biker accustomed to browns.

Nearly 40 percent of the area of Washington and Oregon lie in a high, dry plateau. Trapped in the rain shadow of the Cascades, this land can be a brutally cold or hot host to a biker. If you are prepared, the rewards of riding in this special area are well worth it. Check local conditions before starting out.

One way to prepare is to begin your desert ride just before dawn. If traveling with loud pipes, I suggest you roll your bike away from your sleeping motel before starting it up. From **Bend,** follow the signs to US Highway 20 toward **Burns** and **Ontario.** Instantly after leaving the last gas station and strip mall in Bend, the desert is all around you. The temptation is to really open up the throttle and blast on a dawn-deserted highway, but this is the time many desert animals are active. I suggest you do not exceed your ability to stop if a turtle, deer, or other animals should be resting in the road.

Notice the light, colors, and smells. No one else will. It will be your secret. Don't expect any services in the desert settlements called **Millican, Brothers,** and **Hampton. Riley** is a little over 100 miles from Bend and a place you can stretch your legs. Riley has a motel/café if it's already too hot. By now the freshness of the desert might be changing to a dusty, sage smell. You might be peeling off layers or even wetting your neck cloth and opening jacket vents.

If the heat is not forcing you to hurry on, Burns is worth a stop. You will think you've gone back to the Old West—or at least what people in the 1950s thought the Old West would look like: charming cowboy storefronts, shops, cafés, and an interesting **County Museum** showing cowboy photos, original quilts, and a turn-of-the-century kitchen.

Pulling out of Burns and going toward the **Stinkwater Pass,** you'll notice the landscape slowly changing. The plains reveal more rocky outcrops as you pull out of the 12-million-year-old basalt plateau that nestles Burns. Rock hounds in this part of Oregon have found beautiful fossils and thunder eggs; so much so that the thunder egg is now the official state rock of Oregon. Not wishing to load my bike down with pretty, and even valuable, rocks, I've never taken a serious rock-hunting trip in this part of Oregon.

The last time I rode this road, the heat became so intense during the late morning hours that I found myself constantly stopping to rewet my neck cloth and my clothes under my armored jacket and pants. Bring, and drink, more water than you think is necessary.

Looking down into the Malheur River Valley toward Vale, you realize this part of Oregon is not all flat.

CHAPTER

7

Juntura has a friendly café and RV park called **The Oasis.** You can get lemonade, take off your riding clothes, and rest in a sprinkler near a rustic picnic table while cooling down for the last section into Ontario. This highway did not exist until 1927, when some Juntura folks joined in with small communities all over the sparsely populated parts of Oregon, Northern California, and Idaho to form the Yellowstone Cut-Off Association to grade and build this highway.

When you leave Juntura, you will be treated to some beautiful and dramatic desert scenes. The **Malheur River,** a cold, green thread flowing eastward off the Harney plateau toward the **Snake River,** has cut a deep and winding canyon into the ancient basalt. The canyon walls reveal lively, bright colors of ancient soils streaking the scene with reds, pinks, purples, pale greens, and more browns than anyone knows the name of. Terraces, pinnacles, and rugged vertical towers entertain even a hot biker. Geologists believe the reds tell of a wet tropical climate that existed in these parts during the Miocene time.

I love the road between Juntura and **Vale:** the contrast of the joyful green waters of the Malheur River and the most dramatic desert colors of this trip, the graceful sweeping turns following all the straightness of the early part of the day, and the strong smell of onions and peppermint growing as you approach Vale. Cars travelers do not seem to notice the precious views, smells, and curves. Too bad for them.

My first impression of **Ontario** was not favorable. Perhaps it was because the heat that day was nearly record-setting. Perhaps it was because all the strip malls, chain restaurants, and fast food joints made it look like it had no interesting past. At any rate, the ordinariness of Ontario can be overlooked when a visitor realizes the economic importantance of this gateway city. In the early years, the train tracks stopped here. Near the turn of the century, Ontario was a hub of shipping, opening markets as far east as Omaha to beef and other range products grown in Eastern Oregon. Even today the fertile sedimentary soils, deposited onto the floor of an ancient lakebed, produce onions, beets, and russet potatoes.

When I stay in Ontario, I look for a motel that has a pool and allows me to park my bike right outside my room. Wherever you stay, put something under your kickstand so your bike doesn't sink into the asphalt of the molten parking lot.

If you make it to Ontario and still feel fresh, travel on. Otherwise rest up for a dawn departure to the mysteries of John Day River Valley (Trip 22), perhaps the most intense time-machine ride ever. You may not run into

Surrounded by tall cottonwoods, this stop in Juntura also has an RV park. Here you can wet down your neck cloth and underclothes to prepare for the final run along the Malheur River.

locusts, but you will pass through some of the most geologically interesting places this side of the Grand Canyon.

Distance From Bend To:	
Burns	131 miles (abundant services)
Juntura	189 miles (Food, RV park with showers and shade)
Vale	245 miles (Gas, marginal food and lodging)
Ontario	262 miles (Better food and lodging)

Trp 22 Oregon's Secret Ride

From Ontario to Condon

Distance *250 miles (all day—break this into two rides if it's hot)*

Terrain *Some desert riding conditions. See sidebar page 78 for desert riding suggestions. Mostly hilly open country, some forest hallways with dense trees on both sides, watch for deer, RVs, and a stiff neck from looking everywhere at once*

Highlights *Geological fairyland, more earth colors and fantastic rock formations than you'll ever see—anywhere, finest biking roads in all the Pacific Northwest, friendly rural people, and good food*

Imagine hot pancake syrup bubbling out of a field near your high school. Curious eh? It keeps coming out. You notice that when it cools, it's hundreds of times harder than concrete. It keeps coming. Like syrup, it fills in all the little valleys and cracks. When it hardens, everything below it is sealed away.

Most of this area is range land, but I've seldom seen any cattle out in the desert.

CHAPTER

7

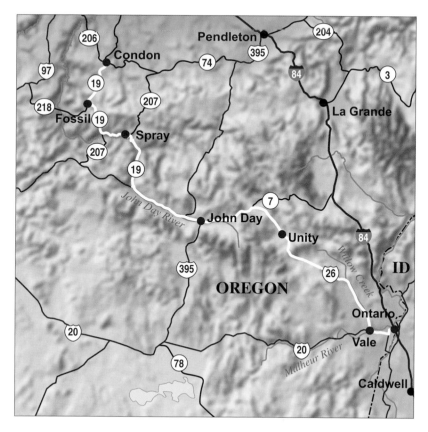

Your high school? Gone. In the Pacific Northwest, this "syrup" was basalt lava. It covered nearly the entire region, sometimes thousands of feet thick. Now and then a volcano would poke through.

The whole character of the region has been shaped by this basalt flow. The canyons, cliffs, hills, and mountains are all the way they are due to this incredibly hard basalt. What kind of geological and biological history is hidden beneath this hard crust? There are few places where we are allowed to lift the basalt skirt and peek at the secrets of the Pacific Northwest's past. The **John Day** area is the best place to peek.

The Route From Ontario

0 From Ontario on Highways 26 and 20 west

165 State Highway 19 toward Spray

249 Arrive in Condon

First Modern Weapons-of-Mass-Destruction Attack

Antelope is a wide place in the road, but locally famous for the 1980s take-over by followers of an eccentric India guru. Red-garbed followers flooded into town, established residency, and voted out the city council. They passed ordinances allowing nudity in the town park and changed the name of the Antelope Café to Zorba the Budda. As members of the cult drifted into paranoia, they launched the first biological attack in modern times by poisoning a salad bar with salmonella bacteria. More than 700 residents of The Dalles got sick as a result. The law finally caught up with the leadership of the cult, it dissolved, and peace was restored to Antelope.

Now you can have a meal at the Antelope Café and chat with the locals about farm prices. If you go on to Shaniko, you can enjoy a tiny town that has decided to dress up like a cowboy. The beautifully restored Shanico Hotel and the false fronted shops nearby give the town an Old West feel.

Looking past the irrigated fields of Cant Ranch, some of the intense dark browns reveal themselves. What's hidden in these hills? More saber-toothed cats? Dog bears? Maybe an ancient artiodactyl?

CHAPTER

7

Notice the various colored layers? Which is the forest, the swamp, the inland sea? So many secrets! Many of the turnouts have interpretive signs which reveal much to the traveler who pauses.

A biker on a journey through this area can see the secrets revealed in geological light shows of earthy colors and naked displays of powerful natural forces. Short hikes, stops at pull-outs, and the **Sheep Rock Unit Museum** allow a traveler to see fossils of saber-toothed cats, dog bears, and other prehistoric animals.

I suggest you begin your journey in the early morning to avoid the heat. Head toward **Vale** on US Highway 26. Once you are at Vale, turn north on US 26 toward John Day. After a steep climb up large, bare hills of eroded sediment, your road begins to follow Willow Creek. Morning shade from the surrounding high bluffs and rocks, as well as the coolness offered by the creek, make this a pleasant journey. At this time of day, the pretty farms offer a green contrast to the browns and golds surrounding them.

You can get breakfast in **Unity,** a town set up to serve the ranchers, hunters, and travelers in the area. During breakfast, you can mentally prepare yourself for the ride through **Picture Canyon.**

Fossils found near this John Day part of Oregon show evidence of life through eons.

Remember basalt? It's hard, right? Then why did the **John Day River** decide to attempt to cut through it? What you have is a narrow, precision-cut gorge through 1500 feet of lava. It's called Picture Gorge because of some ancient Indian pictographs present on the walls. The John Day River and Highway 19 flow swiftly from meadows to valley through this cut.

Be sure to stop at the pull-outs on either side of this gorge. They have interpretive signs and beautiful views of the wonders of the John Day River valley. This persistent river cut away enough of the basalt crusts to reveal the ancient secrets of the area. At various times this place was an ocean bottom, a great fresh water swamp, a parched desert, and a massive forest. Ash falls and mudflows preserved all these secrets. Many experts regard the John Day region as the best place to find and study ancient fossils.

The **Sheep Rock Unit** is a required stop on this journey. Even if fossils of three-toed horses do not get your juices flowing, the restful shade, picnic tables, bathrooms, drinking fountains, and modern horses on the **Cant Ranch** will refresh a tired traveler. I like to lie on the cool, grassy shade gazing at the surrounding cliffs and bluffs. After such a stop, it's easier to concentrate on the roads. The road from US 26 to Sheep Rock Unit is well signed, but you are turning north on Highway 19 toward **Spray.** You will stay on 19 all the way to **Condon.**

Condon has a clean, comfortable strip motel, **The Condon Motel,** on the north edge of town and a grand old hotel, recently restored to a high level of charm and comfort: **Hotel Condon.** The hotel serves high-end cuisine, while across the street, the **Country Café** serves the big, simple meals a farm hand would want. Try their chicken fried steak. The gas station closes at 6 p.m., so get gas before dinner.

Terrific side trips from Condon include the fabulous roads to **Heppner** and **Antelope/Shaniko.** Heppner, a more prosperous town with a population just under 2,000, is twice the size of Condon.

From your base in Condon, you can connect to several of the Trips in this book. Look at the ride to British Columbia (Trip 6) or a terrific ride through the Columbia River Basin (Trip 1). Each one runs across, near, or under old basalt slabs and takes you near views of volcanoes that have managed to pierce the hard crust. There's more to learn here than what you got in high school.

Condon Lodging

Condon Motel
(541) 384-2181

Hotel Condon
(800) 201-6706
www.hotelcondon.com

Trip 23   Christmas Valley Confession

Distance   *226 miles (all day with stops for photos, short hikes, gawking, and meals)*

Terrain   *About two-thirds is flat and straight, some canyon and mountain gentle, sweeping turns. Get an early start to avoid heat and winds and keep your tank topped up.*

Highlights   *Nearly the whole area is so naked of plants, you can see all the geological wonders, including enormous alkaline lakes, tallest fault scarp in North America, dunes, beautiful earth colors and rock formations. Also there are rustic towns, huge cattle ranches, friendly people, and great food.*

Christmas Valley is truly a valley, but that means it is surrounded by high, rocky hills. (Photo by Sharon Hansen)

The Route From Valley Falls

0 mi   From Valley Falls go 61.5 miles north on State Highway 395

61.5   At Christmas Valley/Wagontire Road (also called County Road 514) turn left. This is well marked as toward Christmas Valley

88   If you are staying at the Outback B&B, look for their hand painted sign. Otherwise, continue to the town of Christmas Valley

100   Continue through Christmas Valley. Watch for sign for Fort Rock

113   Turn right toward Fort Rock

129   From Fort Rock, continue west on County Road 511.

135   Turn left (south) onto Fremont Highway toward Silver Lake

226   Arrive back in Valley Falls

CHAPTER
7

Climb up onto Fort Rock and peer out of a slit to view the desert disappearing into the horizon.

It's a story I thought I'd never tell. Perhaps it's best that a suburbanite like me tell it. I've enjoyed riding in every climate the great Pacific Northwest has to offer: the rugged snowcapped mountains, the gentle grasslands, the soggy temperate rainforests, the high dry plains, the lonely coastal fog-shrouded hills, but I've never viewed the desert as anything but an obstacle to where I was going. I'd much rather hang out at Starbucks and watch people watch my bike than head off into the desert.

Perhaps that was because I'd only crossed the Oregon and Washington deserts riding in a car. The heat blast that hit each time the door opened made me long for the cool forests to the west. Then came my first motorcycle desert crossing. Some friends and I had picked what was to be the hottest week in Oregon history to make the journey. I feared the ending of the story before the first chapter began.

Always uncomfortable in high heat, I thought I'd spend my days miserable and bored, looking at mile after mile of sagebrush. As the story unfolded, it became one of the best rides I've ever taken: the naked beauty of the desert,

Fort Rock

Picture a wagon train pursued by hostile Indians. There is no refuge in the desert, or is there? According to legend, the wagon train headed toward a formation called Fort Rock—a natural walled citadel rising 325 feet from the floor of the desert. Recently, several pairs of 9,000-year-old sandals were found in a nearby cave. This interesting rock formation was formed five to six million years ago when volcanic material attempted to rise up from the floor of a lake. Fort Rock puts a visitor in touch with ancient peoples and events. It is a state park now and contains several trails to allow a visitor to explore the views and imagine the geological and human violence that formed the history of this special place. Just outside the park, the community of Fort Rock has a tavern with good food. You can enjoy a chicken dinner and think about the wagon train holding off the Indians.

the silvery dawns, the horizon constantly tugging on my bike. I liked the genuine, flinty people who flourished in the harsh climate.

When it came time to introduce my wife to riding, I chose to take our suburban lives to a world where the word latte is rarely heard and not fully understood: the southeastern high desert area called **Christmas Valley.** Looking at the map, it's a great, upside down triangle that now draws me like some kind of mystery force. Sturgis-bound Californians have long known about this special place.

To get to Christmas Valley from California, turn off from 395 about 62 miles north of **Lakeview.** Take the mostly straight road through sagebrush country, past a giant super secret U.S. spy radar array (please don't tell anyone about it.), and up a steep 8 percent hill to a mountain-enclosed plateau now called Christmas Valley.

Some people think John Fremont named this valley when he camped here on December 24, 1843. The true story is: he camped about 150 miles south of this area and some map maker mistakenly assigned the name to a place Fremont had never visited. The town of Christmas Valley has a lodge, which serves simple hardy meals, and cheap strip motel rooms used mostly by migrant workers and sage rat shooters. These rooms were on the rustic side last time I looked. We stayed in the impossibly clean **Outback Bed and Breakfast** 12 miles east of town. Best breakfast I've ever had.

White mineral deposits ring Lake Abert, a rich source of brine shrimp for migratory birds.

From the town of Christmas Valley, follow the signs west to **Fort Rock** to see one of the few geological wonders in the area accessible by paved roads. Stay alert on the 29 miles from Christmas Valley to Fort Rock. Sometimes these roads take a 90-degree turn for no apparent reason. The straight part can lull a rider into thinking the highway will never turn.

Join State Route 31 just seven miles east of Fort Rock. From the junction, it's 68 miles north to **Bend** or a little over 18 miles to **Silver Lake** if you turn south. To complete the Christmas Valley Triangle, turn south on State Route 31. At the frontier town of Silver Lake, you can drive the four miles to one of the most famous steak houses in Oregon: the **Cowboy Dinner Tree** restaurant: reservations only (541) 576-2426. The steak is known for its 26 to 30 oz. weight—about the size of a football. If you have no way of dealing with leftovers, you might want to save this experience for later and just eat at the **Silver Lake Café and Bar.**

Leaving Silver Lake you will pass by ranches, an abandoned one-room school, and the town of **Summer Lake. The Lodge at Summer Lake** has meals and several simple motel rooms. A couple of miles later you'll find the **Summer Lake Inn Bed and Breakfast,** a more upscale family resort. After you pass the 24 Ranch, you'll see more and more of the alkali portion of Summer Lake, as well as the high brown and gray basalt mountains on the right. These are often snowcapped in winter and spring.

State Route 31 takes you past Summer Lake an into interesting desert floor decorated by volcanic monuments. Twenty-nine miles after Summer Lake you roll into **Paisley.** Named after the town in Scotland, it has had a post office for over 100 years. I like the little city park—perfect for a picnic. Often hunters and fishermen stay at their RV park and motel and eat in their restaurant. When you step into the gas station you will think you've gone back into time—just like the 1950s gas stations my daddy told me about. Closed on Sundays.

On the east side of the triangle that makes this loop, we stopped at the highest and most exquisite fault scarp in North America. Turn to your right; you see a sheer slab of amazingly hard, dark basalt rising abruptly 2,500 feet from the desert floor. Turn to your left; there is a beautiful blue lake surrounded by perfect white alkaline shores. Hundreds of birds gather to feast on the brine shrimp that miraculously survive in the caustic waters. My coffee-shop mind was unable to grasp the terrible and fragile beauty of this desert no matter how often my eyes shouted, "This is beautiful!"

To finish this Christmas Valley triangle, you will motor 23 miles south from Paisley on State Route 31 to **Valley Falls.** Your tale of a desert crossing could have a happy ending like mine. All the yokels at the coffee shop will hang on every word as you tell your desert tale.

Before starting a Christmas Valley story of your own, be aware of local weather conditions: high winds, heat, or frigid night air can affect how your desert story ends. Be aware that the best time to travel is early morning when the winds are usually quiet but the animals are most active. After a windstorm, parts of the highway could be covered with drifted sand or alkali dust. Does this make you want to linger near the neighborhood Starbucks instead of heading out to the desert? I understand.

Food and Lodging

Outback Bed and Breakfast
(541) 420-5229

Christmas Valley Desert Inn
(541) 576-2262

Christmas Valley Lakeside Terrace
(541) 576-2309

CHAPTER

7

Trip 24 Klamath Falls to Burns

Distance *235 miles (one day with rest stops, meals, and photos)*

Terrain *Straight desert highways, canyon sweepers, country roads, and small towns. Main roads are all paved, but many side trips involve gravel. Hazards include weather, winds, farm equipment, and RVs on the the highway, a tendency to go too fast, soft highway shoulders, desert animals (especially near dawn and dusk), and cattle, occasional pot holes and possible rocks and gravel near the base of cliffs and gravel road intersections.*

Highlights *Working cattle ranches, dramatic geological formations, canyons and cliffs, pine forests, mountain views, alkali lakes, deer, antelope, birds, and Oregon's friendliest people*

On a springtime side trip to Lake of the Woods, we found snow. Mt. McLoughlin shines in the background.

CHAPTER

7

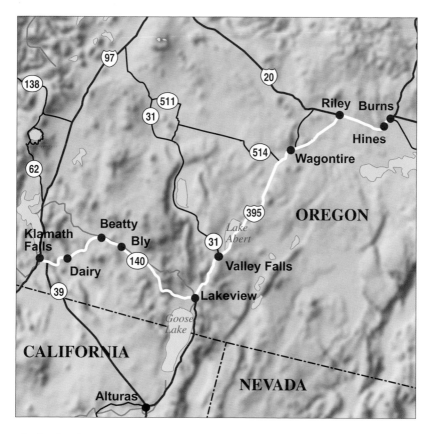

No Starbucks. No micro brews. Credit cards not accepted. Mid-desert gas station closed on Sundays. Bitter, caustic lakes of concentrated minerals. Stubby sage and salt bushes painted gray by dust blowing from dry mineral lake beds. This could make a yuppie on a $20,000 motorcycle long for the suburbs.

The Route From Klamath Falls

0	Leave Klamath Falls going east on Highway 39
6	Turn left onto 140 toward Lakeview
97	At 395 turn left toward Burns
121	At Valley Falls, this could be the last gas for 90 miles
211	Turn right (east) onto Highway 20 toward Burns
238	Arrive in Burns

CHAPTER
7

This is Oregon? This high, flat plateau is often not associated with Oregon.

You might wonder why this trip was included in a book about great journeys in the Pacific Northwest. Most of us Oregonians live on the west side of the state and are curious why anyone would ride 350 miles out into the desert when the mountains and hills around **Portland** offer some outstanding motorcycling roads.

Nearly all Oregonians are ignorant of a reclining beauty in our back yard. Truly the southeastern part of Oregon lies naked in the sun, showing her wonders and secrets to any who bother to look. It is remarkable for its geological and natural wonders, colorful history, friendly people, clean air, and wonderful biking roads. When you switch off your bike, you hear a rare silence that exists in few other places. Life is different here, and the experience is as refreshing as swapping bikes with a buddy when your backside is feeling saddle sore.

I begin this journey in **Klamath Falls,** a growing town about 20 miles from the California border. Now with a whopping population of 40,000, its peaceful downtown belies a history of vigilante violence, range rights battles, and Indian/settler wars. Highwaymen held up stage coaches, and cattle rustlers were as common as Starbucks in suburbia, until the last one was filled with lead. Captain Jack led the Modoc Indians in a bloody uprising and was finally hung at **Fort Klamath.** One of the first white men to see this area, John C. Fremont lost three men to the warlike Klamath Indians. Klamath Falls: one tough town.

At 4,100 feet in elevation, this former Wild West town is hot in summer and bitter cold in winter. You feel like you are in a dry desert town, but this area is all about lakes and thermal hot springs. K Falls, as the locals call it, provides suburban amenities to travelers who take advantage of the terrific biking roads in the area. This journey book gives you a great way to go through this area, but if you can stay a few days, K Falls could make a great hub for exploring the **Fremont National Forest** and the **Sky Lakes Wilderness Area.** You could still have a morning latté.

To begin Trip 24, go east out of town on Highway 39 to State Highway 140. Follow the signs to **Lakeview.** You will see the Klamath Falls' McMansions and a golf course on your left as you leave town. You'll pass through well-maintained farm lands surrounded by rounded, lightly wooded mountains. Small towns like **Dairy, Beatty,** and **Bly** might show rustic charm or rural shabbiness. You'll notice gentle sweeping turns changing to twisties between Beatty and Bly.

About 55 miles out of K Falls, you will roll into the tiny village of Bly. During World War II, the Japanese bombed Bly using explosives attached to balloons. Six Americans were killed during the offensive, five of whom were children. Today you can get gas or groceries in this tiny town and motor your way deeper into Oregon's back yard.

Alkali Lake often dries up. Blowing white minerals coat the upwind side of the desert removing all color. The eerie black and white rocks and bushes surprise strangers.

Mt. McLoughlin dominates the landscape just west of Klamath Lake.

The flat valleys you pass through were formed by sediment deposited when the area was under water five million years ago—an eye blink in geological time. All the hills and mountains were formed by volcanic action. Some of the volcanoes stopped erupting and began to cook their rocks with steam. Such a place is **Quartz Mountain,** an area so rich in mercury and uranium that it was mined in years past.

As you get closer to **Lakeview,** many of the hills and mountains are rounded ash heaps. Some of these look soft, like hippos hiding under thick fuzzy blankets; others are somewhat rocky. They all stand waiting to entertain a traveler who bothers to look.

Many people visit Lakeview just to see its geyser, **Old Perpetual.** It spouts 60 feet every four to ten minutes in the summer. You can find it about two miles north of town near a run-down-looking spa that offers a 107 degree pool—quite a bit cooler than the natural 200-degree water temperature.

I like Lakeview for its charming downtown, and the little park near the courthouse is a nice spot for a picnic. By Lake County standards, Lakeview is a big town, with six motels, several gas stations, restaurants, and abundant rural character. It's common to see cowboys and ranchers on the streets. The grizzled old guy with four days growth of beard and battered cowboy hat might just be a savvy multimillionaire rancher. You'll notice that visitors are welcomed and treated warmly.

You might wonder why it's called Lakeview since no lake is visible anywhere in town. Apparently **Goose Lake,** to the south, was much higher than it is now. Years ago the name Lakeview made more sense. As recent as 1990 the name was used to trick unsuspecting city folks into buying worthless one-acre parcels of "lake front" property. It was lake front all right, just no water.

Twenty-three miles north of Lakeview on US Route 395, you come to **Valley Falls**—a gas station at the intersection of State Route 31 and US Route 395. To get an attendant you might need to enter the store and interrupt a chess game. This is getting closer to the heart of Oregon's backyard.

From Valley Falls, take 395 to the right. Pass through three desert valleys divided by hilly areas. When I see **Albert Rim** rising steeply 2,500 feet above the highway, it makes me wonder if the rim rose up or the valley floor sank in a giant cataclysmic earthquake. **Lake Abert** shines blue and benignly in the sun. Avoid contact with its caustic waters, which offer a false promise of refreshment.

The area is known for petroglyphs and arrow heads, evidence of past civilizations. **Alkali Lake** and **North Alkali Lake** had water last time I was through there, but they may be pretty low or dry at times. Alkali Lake is populated with brine shrimp: a hardy little animal that is often harvested for pet food and feeds thousands of birds.

When you reach the Christmas Valley turnoff (Called County Road 5-14, but never labeled that with a sign that I could find) it's only 30 miles to one of the best bed and breakfast places in Oregon: **Outback Bed and Breakfast.** No better breakfast is available anywhere. The owners, former motorcycle travelers, know how to make a biker feel welcome. Call for reservations, they have only two rooms.

If you press on, you will pass through **Wagontire,** which locals claim to be newly purchased by some city slickers, and on to **Riley.** Riley has food and lodging, but most travelers continue on to **Hines** or **Burns,** which have a rich selection of motels and restaurants.

Some travelers view this great journey as something to be endured in order to get somewhere else. In truth, this trip could be a high point for a Pacific Northeast traveler who bothers to notice what's right there in the back yard.

CHAPTER

7

Desert Riding

This motorcycling paradise can be hell if you are not prepared. Make sure your bike is in top shape. Most of these rural ranchers do their own repairs. You won't find many bike shops. Top up the gas tank often. Gas stations usually close around 6 and may not be open on Sundays. Your cell phone will be 90 percent worthless in this part of Oregon. See the hot weather sidebar on page 78 for gear suggestions. Most importantly, check local weather conditions. This is high desert. Many of the highest passes are choked with snow as late as June. Triple digit daytime temperatures are common in summer. Wind gusts can reach more than 100 mph. Nearly every resident of this area has hit a deer or rabbit near dawn or dusk. Keep your speed down and caution levels up. The roads are mostly in great shape with the exception of occasional rough pavement and some odd pot holes here and there. Often the shoulders are quicksand.

Burns/Hines Lodging

Best Inn Motel
(541) 573-1700

Bontemps Motel
(541) 573-2037

Burns RV Park
(541) 573-7640

Comfort Inn
(541) 573-3370

Days Inn
(541) 573-2047

Lakeview Lodging

Rim Rock Motel
(541) 947-2185

Best Western Skyline Motor Lodge
(541) 947-2194

Lakeview Lodge Motel
(541) 947-2181

Snyder's Motel
(541) 947-2282

Klamath Falls Lodging

Quality Inn
(541) 882-4666

Econo Lodge
(541) 884-7735

Oregon 8 Motel and RV Park
(541) 883-3431

Outback Bed and Breakfast
(541) 420-5229
http://twohicks.mystarband.net/

CHAPTER

7

Deuce-and-a-Half

At 11 years old, I'd lived my whole life in the suburbs. My family drove to the mountains for a camping trip. Daddy told me I was in charge of firewood. First I had to learn to master the ax. Putting the blade into the wood at just the right angle to pull a big chip away from the log became my quest. My mother told me later that she'd never seen me so puffed up with pride when the ranger complimented our woodpile.

The Great Pacific Northwest is my woodpile now. I love riding this country. Perhaps the feeling of accomplishment is the reason to take this 14-day ride. Perhaps the joy of seeing geological wonders, deep forests, wild coasts, smoking volcanoes, meeting friendly people and enjoying great food is a better reason. Some people ride just to photograph this beauty. Just like it takes a certain skill to pull a big wood chip away from a log, a biker enjoys exercising and refining certain riding skills. Whatever your reason for taking this ride, you'll never forget it and long to repeat it.

A dawn journey into the golden hills near John Day is worth repeating.

264

It's a good idea to have a riding buddy when traveling the most remote parts of the Pacific Northwest.

Think about it: 2,500 miles through one of the most beautiful places on earth. This is a chance to ride the famous coastal highways from redwoods to Washington's Long Beach Peninsula. Riding the Olympic Peninsula and exploring the unearthly Hoh Rainforest. Soaking in the charm of ferry travel to Vancouver Island's best roads. Exploring the amazing climate variations of Western British Columbia: spicy fir forests, glowing blue glaciers, red desert rock outcrops, and the grand **Fraser River Canyon.**

Next time you are at a rest stop and someone says, "What's so great about Canadian roads?" You can give them chapter and verse about all the secrets you've discovered.

I remember going into an old dusty file cabinet to find a certain slide for this book. Once I began looking through the old pictures, the images took me to long-forgotten, cherished places. Hours later I emerged in a dream state without the slide I came for. Perhaps you will set out on this Deuce-and-a-Half to try out a certain road, restaurant, or experience, just to find yourself pulled into a world that seems created just for you. When you read the chapter on this great journey, you will notice I urge you to enjoy where you are at in the trip.

CHAPTER

8

From Canada, you get to probe one of the least visited but most beautiful National Parks: **North Cascade National Park.** There was no paved road through this area until 1977 so it can become your special national park.

Before leaving, be sure to study the chapter to find out how to prepare for the trip. Print out ferry schedules and take care of other similar details mentioned in the chapter. Make sure you pack this book to keep useful addresses, maps, commentary, and suggestions.

When you return from this glorious trip, you will look at what you've accomplished with pride. You deserve the pride—few have ever created such a woodpile before.

The Middle Fork of the Smith River, just south of the Oregon border, appears rugged and isolated.

Trip 25 Deuce-and-a-Half

The Whole Pacific Northwest in 14 Days and 2,500 Miles

Before starting this 2,500 mile journey you will need to decide if you are capable of such a trip. Ask yourself if you can average 200 miles a day for 14 days. Many bikers find this an exhausting pace. Is not the point of a motorcycle vacation to relax and enjoy one's time on the bike?

Think of the Pacific Northwest as a one-trip buffet featuring wonderful, as well as ordinary, foods. Should you take a small portion of everything? Would it be better just to take some of what you know you are going to like? What if you taste something that is so good, it's all you want to eat? Since your plate was full, you only had room for a small amount. To ride this 14-day trip, you are committing to take a little of everything.

Pausing at Duffy Lake in British Columbia, we take a scenery break. (Photo by Sharon Hansen)

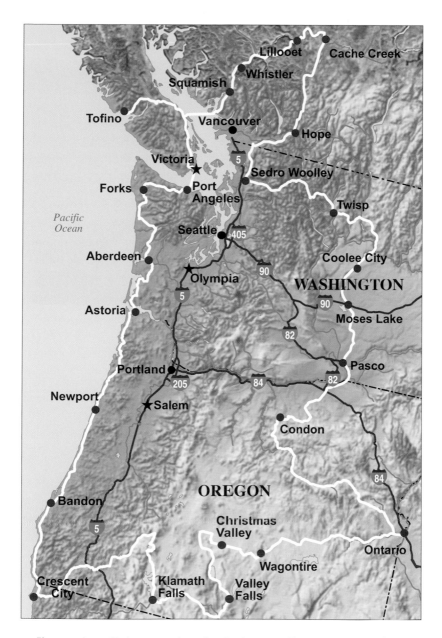

I'm putting all these cautionaries in because I want you to enjoy the Pacific Northwest as much as I do. It'd be sad to have you finish your trip exhausted from 100 hours in a helmet, with only a glance at some of what we locals love so much about the Pacific Northwest.

The Astoria Bridge stretches beautifully across the Columbia River. Running across this span can be quite a thrill.

I came up with 14 days because two weeks is what most people have for a vacation. It would be easy to lop off part of this trip if you had less time or decided to linger at the Oregon Coast. The whole route is just over 2,500 miles if you count side trips. Side trips are not factored in on the daily mileage counts. This means if you ride six hours a day at an average speed of 40 mph, you should make the whole loop with time to spare.

You might be thinking that you can easily go 40 mph, but remember when you are sitting in a restaurant, getting gas, or taking a picture, you are going 0 mph. To make this up, you'll need to ride longer than six hours or faster than 40 mph. Some places on this ride, you will be sorely pressed to achieve more than 40 mph: along the Sea to Sky Highway from Vancouver to Whistler, for example. Other times heat or windy conditions will limit your speed and time in the saddle. (See hot weather riding sidebar on page 78)

If you're tired or find yourself in a heavenly place, I suggest you abandon the Deuce-and-a-Half and enjoy the portion of the Pacific Northwest you are able to sample. Spend an extra day in the same motel or campground and relax. Link up to another journey in this book and come back from your vacation relaxed and in love with motorcycle travel.

CHAPTER

8

Besides deciding if this trip is right for you, you'll need to make sure your bike is up to the trip. Ninety hours is a long time to be sitting on a noisy, vibrating machine. If your bike is uncomfortable or unreliable, you may want to put it on a trailer, tow it from Pacific Northwest destination to destination, then take small tours. I've seen many couples doing this. Another choice is to rent a comfortable bike from one of the rental places mentioned in this book

Perhaps the most important element for a successful Deuce-and-a-Half is your motorcycling proficiency level. Examine your motorcycle skills. If you are new to riding or otherwise lack skills, I suggest you develop your skills before undertaking a big trip like this. Take classes through the Motorcycle Safety Foundation and read up on the subject. Two of my favorite books are *Proficient Motorcycling* by David Hough, and *Smooth Riding the Pridmore Way* by Reg Pridmore.

Let's say you have the time, the skills, the will, and the bike for the trip. I explained this ride as a clockwise route up the Oregon Coast to British Columbia, down through eastern Washington and Oregon, over to Crater Lake and finally back to the coast. You could plug into this ride from anywhere on the circle and ride it counterclockwise. If the heat is hammering Eastern Oregon and Washington, stick to the coast first and hope that the heat abates before you come down the eastern spine of the Pacific Northwest. Likewise, if the weather is perfect on the east side while rain is pounding the coast, head east first.

The prow of an Native American Canoe points to the valley near the mouth of the Columbia River.

CHAPTER

8

Each day get an early start to avoid traffic. Take this book with you; it contains motel and other phone numbers that can be helpful. You might want to remove the maps from this book for your tank bag window. Carry additional state and provincial maps on this trip. The publisher and I do not take responsibility for any errors on our maps. I think they are great maps, but have others handy.

Before taking a leg of this trip, read the chapter on that area to learn about the region, side trips, travel techniques, and places to eat and stay. Find out the typical hazards associated with the leg you are riding.

Before leaving, print out ferry schedules for Port Angeles to Victoria and Nanaimo to Vancouver. Ferry contact information is available at the end of this chapter.

Enjoy your trip. After sampling these items on the tray, you may find yourself coming back again and again to regain the feelings you have on this trip. Kind of like taking a nap so you can get back into a sweet dream you had the previous night. You might also want to strike out into some of the many places not mentioned in this book.

Joffre Park along Duffy Lake Road offers views of glowing, blue glaciers.

CHAPTER

8

Day 1: Crescent City to Newport

You can ride this six-hour day quite easily if the weather cooperates or the scenery does not capture you. On a weekend or near summer holidays, you should call ahead for reservations. Try to pull off the highway before four o'clock to be sure to get a room if you have no reservations.

If you are making good time, consider the ride to Cape Arago just north of Bandon. Details in Trip 10.

232 miles

Day 2: Newport to Aberdeen

The northern part of the Oregon Coast is much more congested than the southern part. Allow more time for this leg. If you get an early start, you will be rewarded with more easy miles. You will be going slowly through coastal towns and possibly crawling behind RVs. After you get past Astoria, the highway becomes much faster.

215 miles

Day 3: Aberdeen to Port Angeles

It makes me sad to think you are missing the Hoh Rain Forest and Cape Flattery. You might want to take an extra day here. Even so, this is a low-mileage-day. If you get an early start and take a room in Forks instead of Port Angeles, you can have a picnic lunch in the Hoh Rain Forest or some great clam chowder at Neah Bay. Day Four will be a long day, so get an early start. You want to catch the 8:20 ferry from Port Angeles to Victoria.

164 miles

Day 4: Port Angeles to Tofino

Before crossing the strait from Port Angeles to Victoria, check the ferry schedule. Usually a motorcycle only needs to arrive 30 minutes before departure (cars often park on the dock overnight), but you might not want to cut this voyage too close. Often summer ferries out of Port Angeles are fully booked. During the summer, you have four chances a day to catch a ferry to Victoria. Typically summer ferry times are something like: 8:20 a.m., 1 p.m., 5 p.m., and 9:30 p.m. The ferry ride is usually about two hours and costs about $20. Bring a birth certificate or passport whenever you enter Canada.

As soon as you are off the ferry, follow the signs for Highway 1 going north to Nanaimo.

A Christmas Valley dawn turns everything pewter.

Expect this to be a slow travel day. Grab a spot on the 8:20 ferry. For some reason, it always takes longer to get places in Canada. You are nuts to think you can get a place to stay in Tofino without a reservation. Lots of bikers are nuts so here's what you do if you don't book ahead. As you near the junction of the road to Ucluelet and Tofino (about 35 kilometers from Tofino), you'll see a visitor center for the Pacific Rim National Park. This visitor center, in addition to distributing park information, has a list of all the available rooms in town. You won't get a recommendation about which room is better, but this is the best way I know of getting a last-minute room or campsite in Tofino.

If you have a couple of extra days, I highly recommend the coastal run up Highway 19a to Campbell River and then going west on Highway 28 to Stathcona Provincial Park and Gold River. The ride to Gold River is 220 miles one way from Tofino. Highway 19a runs through small coastal towns. Like my eighth-grade girlfriend, slow but pretty. Then it's a 260-mile trip to get to Whistler and connect to Day 5.

207 miles (If you skip the Gold River side trip.)

Day 5: Tofino to Whistler

This is another long day. You have a 95-minute ferry ride from Nanaimo to Horseshoe Bay, lots of slow roads in remote areas. If you haven't booked ahead, look over the coupons for Whistler accommodations while on the ferry and call from out of town. Last time I did this, I found one that took $20 off the price of my room. It's not cheap, but I think it's fun to stay in Whistler Village to people-watch.

190 miles

Day 6: Whistler to Cache Creek to Hope

After this day, you will have really put on some miles. Travel is slow at first due to the spectacular scenery and twisty road. From Lillooet to Cache Creek, you are on sweeping desert highways with higher speed limits. A wonderful short cut is to take Highway 12 out of Lillooet to Lytton, then stay on Highway 1 to Hope. This cuts Cache Creek from your trip.

255 miles

Tank Bag Secret

There is some motorcycle knowledge denied to those of us who love cruisers—the tank bag. Ever concerned lest our beautiful bike looks dumpy or our perfect paint gets micro scratches, we never look into traveling with a tank bag. If you already use one, you can stop reading here; otherwise drink from the fountain of knowledge.

It started when my wife wanted to take her hiking boots on a trip. I'd already packed the bike. Each tiny space was completely stuffed. To take those hiking boots, I'd need to put on my rain gear and cold weather gloves and leave my camera at home. Instead of doing all that, I picked up an expandable Givi bag. After repacking everything, Sharon had her boots.

We started out on our trip with my map right in front of me, in a clear plastic window at the top pf the tank bag. Of course it's not safe to study it when in motion, but it's right there at every stop. My sunglasses, wallet, camera, water bottle, cell phone, and other necessities are right there, too. At a stop, the whole bag comes with us into the restaurant or visitor center. Pull up to a ferry kiosk, the wallet is right there.

At the end of the trip, I could not find any scratches in my gas tank, but if there were, a little polish would make them invisible. Think about the convenience of a tank bag before trying a long trip. I've converted.

Day 7: Hope to Twisp

When you leave Hope going west toward Vancouver, look for Highway 11 going south as you approach Abbotsford. Signs will say "U.S. Border." Expect it to be slow going through the suburban streets of Abbotsford.

Once in the United States, head south on highway 9 to Sedro Woolley. From here you turn east on Highway 20 through the spectacular North Cascades National Park. I set Twisp as your stop for the night, but it might be fun to spend the night in Winthrop, the Old West-themed town.

232 miles

Day 8: Twisp to Pasco

The first part of this journey will make your heart sing with its views of the remains of the Lake Missoula flood (Trip 6) and the Columbia River Basin. The tank bag directions take you to Coulee Dam and along stunning geological formations. Later, the ride turns into hot, straight roads as you approach Pasco—my least favorite place on this whole journey. I picked Pasco because of its distance from Twisp. If you are feeling fresh, continue on to Heppner or Condon for the night. An early start helps you get your miles in before the heat starts with full ferocity. Check the weather forecast for winds and temperature.

229 miles

Now a source of endless fun for bikers, the low lands of Hoods Canal were formed by massive glaciers.

Sheeprock near John Day has more colors than any rocks should.

Day 9: Pasco to Kimberly

These are my favorite roads of the whole trip. You might arrive at Kimberly, shower, and ride back to Condon (65 miles) just for the chicken fried steak at the Country Café and another chance at these roads. If you make reservations, the nice people at Lands Inn Bed and Breakfast and Airstrip will fire up the kitchen and cook you dinner. If Kimberly is all booked up, call The Fish House Inn in Dayville, 26 miles on down the road, or run the 17 beautiful miles up to Monument. They have a sportsman's motel, café, and tavern. This is a stop I would book ahead since it's pretty much out in the middle of nowhere. Let someone in a car drive another 60 miles to John Day for a room.

 196 miles

Day 10: Kimberly to Ontario

If this road doesn't make you wish you'd studied geology more, nothing will. Stop at the pullouts and the Sheeprock Unit of the John Day Fossil Beds National Monument. In this valley, the basalt crust, covering practically the whole Pacific Northwest, parts to allow travelers a peek up the skirts of time. Watch out for heat. Start early.

 188 miles

Morning mist makes typical Oregon beach trees seem special and somehow more important than the ordinary trees at home. Time to head for the beach.

Day 11: Ontario to Christmas Valley

My experience is that if I start early before winds and heat can really exhaust me, this ride is a highlight. (See desert riding techniques sidebar on page 260.) I'm sending you to Christmas Valley so you can see Fort Rock the next day. If you are not that interested in Fort Rock, go from Ontario to Lakeview (270 miles). Lakeview offers more lodging choices than Christmas Valley. You also get to ride along sand dunes, alkali lakes, and Albert Rim. Remember the basalt skirt? Albert Rim shows it's nearly 3,000 feet thick by revealing an uplifting of the valley floor.

233 miles

Day 12: Christmas Valley to Fort Rock to Klamath Falls

Once again, start early and enjoy the ride to Fort Rock, along the shores of
Summer Lake, past the geyser at Lakeview, then through the hills and forests
of Highway 140 to Klamath Falls.

198 miles

Day 13: Klamath Falls to Crater Lake to Grants Pass

This is a low-mileage day, because you are going to want to spend time at
Crater Lake. It's too grand and blue to just drive past. If you are feeling
rushed, make a run around the west side of Rim Drive, pop out on the north
entrance road, and turn west to run to Grants Pass. This is what the tank bag
directions assume.

At the end of this ride, you will be heading into afternoon sun. It can be
brutal on a hot day. Resist the temptation to ride too far this day. Grants Pass
has nice, cheap motels downtown. The motel clerk will tell you where to
walk for good food.

*These hills near the Tygh Valley of Oregon just become increasingly dramatic as you
approach the Deschutes River.*

CHAPTER

8

The worst part of any journey is the end; you are tired, thinking about getting back to your normal routine, and your seat hurts. Take this day with a relaxed attitude and avoid trying to get home all at once when you are tired and distracted.

180 miles

Day 14: Grants Pass to Crescent City

You might wonder that I plan an 80-mile day. It seems to me that not everyone taking the The Deuce-and-Half-Ride will be from Crescent City. Therefore I've left you some wiggle room to get along on your journey.

Once you are near Crescent City, explore the redwoods. The groves seem to possess holiness; you may find yourself whispering when among them.

85 miles

Dry Falls: this geological wonder lies just off the highway. As I was taking this shot, I heard a big group of bikers blast by, unaware of this feast for the eyes and mind.

I'm not one for camping in the desert, but plenty of travelers do it. It was 106 degrees the day I took this picture of the hot springs camping near Paisley, Oregon.

The Route from Crescent City

Day 1

0 Leave Crescent City going North on Highway 101

232 Arrive in Newport

Day 2

0 Leave Newport going north on 101

215 Arrive in Aberdeen

Day 3

0 Leave Aberdeen going north on 101

110 Arrive in Forks; if continuing on to Port Angeles, continue on 101

169 Arrive in Port Angeles

Day 4

0 Leave Port Angeles on ferry to Victoria

1 When you leave the ferry, follow signs to Highway 1 toward Nanaimo

CHAPTER
8

Sunset comes to Long Beach Peninsula.

62   Go north on Highway 1 to Highway 19

82   Leave 19 to get onto Highway 4

180   Take Highway 4 all the way to Tofino.

Day 5

0   Leave Tofino, retracing your route back to Nanaimo on Highway 4

98   Take Highway 19 toward Nanaimo. Follow all ferry signs

103   Board ferry to Horseshoe Bay

104   Go north on Highway 99

168   Arrive in Whistler

Day 6

0   Leave Whistler on 99 going north

128   Turn south onto Caribou Highway toward Cache Creek

135   At Cache Creek, go south onto Highway 1

187   At Lytton, continue south on Highway 1

255   Arrive in Hope

CHAPTER
8

Day 7

0	Leave Hope behind and go west on Highway 1
49	Turn south onto Highway 11 toward U.S. Border. After crossing this turns into Highway 9
96	At Sedro Woolley, turn east onto Highway 20
232	Arrive in Twisp

Day 8

0	Leave Twisp going south on 20
30	Turn north onto 97
36	Turn south onto 155
115	Turn east onto Highway 2
119	Go south onto Highway 17
205	Merge onto 395 going south
229	Follow signs to Pasco/Highway 12

Tatoosh Island is just off Cape Flattery and about the farthest northwest an American can go and still be in the lower 48.

CHAPTER
8

Day 9

0	Leave Pasco going south on Highway 12
18	Go south onto 730
37	Turn south onto Highway 207
92	Highway 207 turns into 207/206
103	Stay straight on 206 toward Condon
132	At Condon, turn south onto 19
196	Arrive in Kimberly

Day 10

0	Leave Kimberly going south on 19
19	Turn east onto Highway 26 (stop at the J.D. Fossil National Mon.)
190	Arrive in Ontario

Day 11

0	Get on Highway 20 going west toward Burns
158	Turn left onto Highway 395 south at Riley

While eating a terrific dinner in Campbell River on the east side of Vancouver Island, we watched the channel traffic. If you can manage a side trip up here and then west to Strathcona Provincial Park—you've got a great side trip.

CHAPTER

8

195   Follow signs to Christmas Valley

234   Arrive at Christmas Valley

Day 12

0   Head west on Christmas Valley/Wagontire Road. Follow signs to Fort Rock

29   At Fort Rock continue west

37   Turn left toward Silver Lake onto Highway 31

133   At Lakeview, turn west onto Highway 140

229   Arrive in Klamath Falls

Day 13

0   Leave Klamath Falls on 97 going north

23   Veer left onto Highway 62 toward Crater Lake

76   Run around Rim Drive to the north entrance

85   Turn left (west) onto 138

87   Go south onto 230

101   Continue south onto 62

145   Turn west onto 234 toward Gold Hill

160   Get onto Interstate 5 going north toward Grants Pass

175   Take the Grants Pass exit and follow signs to downtown area for motels and good food

Day 14

0   Leave Grants Pass going south on 99 to 199

5   Turn south onto 199

Lodging Information Not Available in Other Chapters

Day 7 Lodging

Blue Spruce Motel and RV
(509) 997-5000

Methow Valley Inn
(509) 997-2253
mvinn@mymethow.com

CHAPTER
8

Day 8 Lodging

Pasco Motels
(800) 359-4827
(Cheapest)

Red Lion Hotel Pasco
(800) 359-4827

Sleep Inn Pasco
(800) 359-4827

Day 9 Lodging

Fish House Inn Bed and Breakfast
(541) 987-2124
(888) 286-FISH

Lands Inn Bed and Breakfast and Airstrip
(541) 934-2333
(Dinner—reservations only)

Monument Motel and RV Park
(541) 934-2242

Day 11 Lodging

Outback Bed and Breakfast
(541) 420-5229

Christmas Valley Desert Inn
(541) 576-2262

Christmas Valley Lakeside Terrace
(541) 576-2309

Index

Other Touring Guides in
The Motorcycle Journeys Series

Motorcycle Journeys Through The Alps and Corsica

Motorcycle Journeys Through The Appalachians

Motorcycle Journeys Through Baja

Motorcycle Journeys Through California

Motorcycle Vagabonding In Japan

Motorcycle Journeys Through Northern Mexico

Motorcycle Journeys Through Southern Mexico

Motorcycle Journeys Through The Southwest

Motorcycle Journeys Through Texas

Motorcycle Journeys Through New England

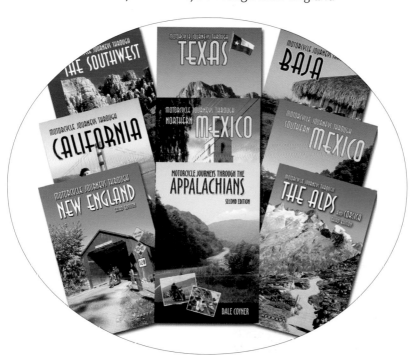

About the Author

Bruce Hansen burns with a love of motorcycling and possesses an impulsive curiosity that causes him to take random turns. From the thousands of dead ends he's encountered, trust in the whims of his riding buddies, hours of research, and just plain luck, he has located the best motorcycle roads in the Pacific Northwest.

After starting his motorcycling life on the seat of a rented 1966 Bridgestone 50, the first bike he owned was a Honda 350 Scrambler. From there he's saddled up various Harleys, BMWs, Hondas, and now his favorite mount: a 1999 Valkyrie. "It's got power, performance and reliability: the three supports that make motorcycle travel so rewarding."

Bruce has been a contributor to various motorcycle magazines, including *Motorcycle Cruiser, Rider, RoadBike, American Iron,* and *Motorcycle Voyager.* When he's not on his bike, behind his camera, or in front of his computer, he teaches a distance writing class through Portland State University (PDX). His favorite job is to teach his fifth grade students each morning in Beaverton, Oregon. His wife, Sharon, and two grown daughters are the light of his life.

For questions, suggestions, or comments about *Motorcycle Journeys Through the Pacific Northwest,* contact Bruce at www.mjpnw.com.